THE ASIAN FINANCIAL CRISIS
The challenge for social policy

THE ASIAN FINANCIAL CRISIS

The challenge for social policy

EDDY LEE

INTERNATIONAL LABOUR OFFICE · GENEVA

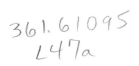

Lee, Eddy
The Asian financial crisis: The challenge for social policy
Geneva, International Labour Office, 1998

/Economic recession/, /Unemployment/, /Social implication/, /Indonesia/, /Korea R./, /Thailand/. 03.04.3
ISBN 92-2-110850-3

ILO Cataloguing in Publication Data

Cover photographs: Crisis on the Asian stock exchange; Crowds push for cheap sugar in Jakarta
© Chris Stowers/Panos Pictures

Printed in Switzerland   WEI/PUB

CONTENTS

ACKNOWLEDGEMENTS

My thanks are due, first of all, to David Freedman and Ali Taqi who encouraged me to embark on this venture. I also owe a special debt of gratitude to Judy Rafferty for having trawled the Web so efficiently and cheerfully on my behalf, to Vincenzo Spiezia for producing the background papers on which section 4.4 is based, and to Geraldeen Fitzgerald for her deft editing of the manuscript. Duncan Campbell was kind enough to provide material on Thailand, and Xiaolun Sun did the data analysis for Chapter 1. In addition, Sriyan de Silva, Bob Kyloh and Frans Roselaers provided very helpful comments on the manuscript. To all of them, my sincere thanks.

THE ASIAN FINANCIAL CRISIS: THE CHALLENGE FOR SOCIAL POLICY

THE CRISIS

1

1.1 INTRODUCTION

Fourteen months since the onset of the Asian financial crisis in July 1997, grave anxiety still prevails in global financial markets. What began as an apparently localized currency and financial crisis in Thailand soon spread to other South-East Asian countries, notably Indonesia, Malaysia and the Philippines. By October that year the crisis had also spread to the Republic of Korea and Hong Kong, China. In spite of this, initial perceptions greatly underestimated the potential severity of the crisis and its contagion effects, both within and beyond the region. Until April 1998 it had been widely thought that the worst impact of the crisis would be confined to the three countries with IMF programmes, namely, Thailand, Indonesia and the Republic of Korea. Moreover, even in these countries the forecasts of the impact on the real economy were that there would be zero or, at worst, a slight decline in GDP in 1998 followed by a moderate recovery in 1999. All other countries in the region, even those that had suffered similar levels of currency depreciation and asset price deflation, were expected to have lower but still significantly positive growth. The potential impact of the crisis on other emerging market economies and on the industrialized countries was deemed to be negligible.

Since April, the actual turn of events has belied the initial optimism. First, the economic downturn in the three worst-affected countries was deeper than expected in the first two quarters of this year. This led to sharp downwards adjustments of the earlier GDP forecasts. In Indonesia GDP is now forecast to decline by 15 per cent while the corresponding figures for Thailand and Korea are now 6.5 and 5 per cent respectively. This contrasts sharply with the forecasts of positive growth of 1 to 2 per cent for these countries that had been made at the end of 1997. Second, the contagion effects within the region have proved to be much stronger. Malaysia and Hong Kong, China, slid into recession in the first two quarters of this year and are now forecast to have negative growth of −4 and −3 per cent respectively for the full year, compared to earlier forecasts of positive growth of 2 to 3 per cent. Similarly, growth forecasts for Singapore, the Philippines, Viet Nam and China have all been revised downwards. Third, the effects of the crisis beyond the region have also proved to be stronger than anticipated. Apart from the dramatic financial collapse in Russia in August, currency and stock markets in emerging markets such as South Africa, Venezuela and Brazil have come under severe pressure. Even the industrialized countries have been affected in the form of recession in Japan and sharp falls in equity prices in the United States and Europe.

The key events that provoked this general turn for the worse in Asia were the political turmoil in Indonesia in April and May and the steadily worsening economic news from Japan. The onset of recession in Japan, together with a significant weakening in the yen, had a large negative impact on East and South-East Asian countries owing to the predominance of that country in the regional economy. Prior to this there had been hopeful signs of stabilization in currency markets and some recovery in stock markets in the first three months of the year.

1.2 EXTENT OF THE CRISIS

It is by now clear that several South-East and East Asian countries have experienced an economic shock of unprecedented severity after decades of uninterrupted high growth. The enormity of the shock is captured by the fact that in the worst-affected countries, namely Thailand, Indonesia and the Republic of Korea, real GDP growth has turned abruptly from over 7 per cent per annum to negative (see table 1.1). In Thailand growth fell from 6 per cent in 1996 to almost zero in 1997, with all the decline

Table 1.1. GDP growth (%)

	1990	1991	1992	1993	1994	1995	1996	1997					1998 (actual)		1998 forecasts					1999 forecasts		
								Q1	Q2	Q3	Q4	Year on year	Q1	Q2	IMF	Govt.	EIU	MS	UBS	Govt.	IMF	UBS
Thailand	11.6	8.1	8.2	8.5	8.9	8.7	6.4					−0.4	−8		−6.5	−7.0	−6.0		−11.0	"Modest recovery"		−3.3
Indonesia	9.0	8.9	7.2	7.3	7.5	8.2	8.0	8.5	6.8	2.5	1.4	4.6	−6.2		−13.5	−10 to −15		−15.0	−17.2	"Bottom out"		−5.5
Korea, Rep. of	9.5	9.1	5.1	5.8	8.6	8.9	7.1	5.6	6.6	6.1	4.0	5.5	−3.9	−6.6	−5.0	−4.0	−7.9		−8.0	"Recovery"	0.0	0.1
Malaysia	9.6	8.6	7.8	8.3	9.2	9.5	8.6	8.5	8.4	7.4	6.9	7.8	−2.8	−6.8	−4.0	−1.0 to −2.0	−3.5		−4.7			−2.6
Philippines	3.0	−0.6	0.3	2.1	4.4	4.8	5.7	5.5	5.6	5.0	4.8	5.1	1.7		1.0	3.0	1.4		0.8	5.0		1.8
Viet Nam	4.9	6.0	8.6	8.1	8.8	9.5	9.3								4.0							
Singapore	9.0	7.3	6.2	10.4	10.5	8.8	7.0	4.0	8.5	10.6	7.7	7.8	5.6		0.5		−0.5		−0.7		1.5	1.5
Hong Kong, China	3.4	5.1	6.3	6.1	5.4	3.9	4.9	5.9	6.8	6.0	2.7	5.3	−1.9	1.9	−3.0		−2.0		−2.5		1.9	−0.5
China	3.8	9.2	14.2	13.5	12.6	10.5	9.7					8.8			5.5				−6.0		5.0	
Japan	5.1	3.8	1.0	0.3	0.6	1.5	3.9					0.8			−1.7	−1.7			−1.4		1.1	0.5
Taiwan															4.0				4.8		4.3	5.2

Sources: International Monetary Fund (IMF): *World Economic Outlook*, Mar. and Oct. 1998; *World Economic Outlook*, Interim Assessment, Dec. 1997; *The Economist* Intelligence Unit (EIU): *Country Risk Service*, 1st, 2nd and 3rd quarters 1998 and 4th quarter 1997; Morgan Stanley; United Bank of Switzerland (UBS), Warburg Dillon Read, *Asian Adviser*, 7 Sept. 1998.

concentrated in the second half of that year, and is projected to fall by at least a further 5 per cent in 1998. In Indonesia the corresponding swing is from 8 per cent growth up to the third quarter of 1997 to a likely absolute decline of 15 per cent in 1998. Such shifts in GDP of the order of 10 per cent or more in one year in relation to what it would have been according to long-standing trends are very severe indeed.

These aggregate income shifts reflect the impacts of precipitous currency devaluations and falls in equity prices which created economic upheaval in their wake (see figures 1.1 and 1.2). The huge devaluations of up to 80 per cent in the worst case (the Indonesian rupiah) caused severe import compression in these open economies and pushed up inflation rates. The fall in equity and other asset prices further depressed

Figure 1.1   Exchange rates index, end period, US$/local currency

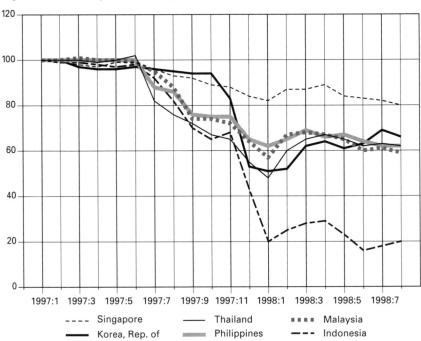

Source: *The Economist*, various issues.

demand through the negative wealth effect. As will be discussed below, these developments caused a sharp fall in output, consumption and average incomes.

Of greater concern than these general negative impacts were those with distributional consequences. Foremost among these was the impact on unemployment and poverty. The most severely affected countries have all experienced massive lay-offs and a sharp rise in unemployment as the currency and financial crises impacted on the real economy. In the absence of unemployment benefits and social assistance, this inflicts severe economic hardship, way above that suggested by the fall in GDP, on job losers and new job seekers. Together with falling real earnings of low-paid workers, this will reverse the impressive trends in poverty

Figure 1.2   Stock market index, end period

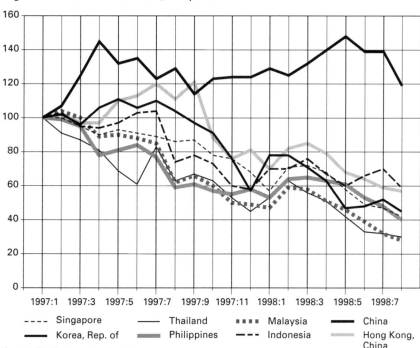

Source: *The Economist*, various issues.

reduction achieved in these countries prior to the crisis. Over and above these primary causes there are other factors making for a rise in poverty, such as an increase in the prices of essential goods and tighter constraints on social expenditures.

The key factor behind this currency and stock market collapse was a massive reversal of foreign capital flows. It has been estimated that for Indonesia, the Republic of Korea, Thailand, Malaysia and the Philippines net private inflows dropped from US$93 billion to –12 billion — a swing of 11 per cent of GDP between the end of 1996 and the end of 1997. This swing in foreign capital flows has continued into 1998.

This financial collapse soon began to impact on the real economy through two main channels. One was a sharply increased fragility in banking systems due to heavy exposure to unhedged short-term foreign loans (especially in Thailand), and to the further decapitalization effect of the fall in domestic asset prices. The other was a debt crisis in corporate sectors similarly exposed to foreign loans (especially in the Republic of Korea and Indonesia). These effects were particularly strong given the high debt-to-equity ratio in many large companies in the pre-crisis period and the high level of domestic bank lending to the private sector in these countries. Apart from this direct impact on foreign-indebted banks and companies, second-round effects soon spread to other parts of the real economy. The banking crisis, together with rising interest rates, resulted in a contraction of credit and a disruption of normal financial intermediation that put even otherwise viable firms under pressure. Difficulties in obtaining working capital and export letters of credit are two often-cited examples of these pernicious effects. Such disruptions in financial intermediation are believed to have prevented firms from reaping the full benefits of the sharp currency devaluations. This financial disruption effect was compounded by the knock-on effects on suppliers and other firms linked to the initial group of troubled companies.

The virulence of this impact on the real economy is seen in the abrupt swing in GDP growth rates described earlier. The effects are by no means over, given that many firms are still teetering on the brink of illiquidity and insolvency and may not survive for long without the successful restoration of confidence in markets.

A striking feature of the present Asian crisis is the extent of market overreaction in terms of the degree to which the currencies have depreciated and asset prices have fallen. The exchange rates and market values of many companies are still at levels that cannot easily be justified by economic fundamentals. It is also clear that stabilization is taking longer than in similar crises in the past and sentiment in international financial markets towards the most affected countries has not yet turned around. Moreover, as mentioned earlier, exports have not yet grown to the extent that was to have been expected in relation to the sharp devaluations.

It is important to note at this stage that there are significant differences among countries in South-East and East Asia both in terms of their pre-crisis situation and policies and in the extent to which they have been hit by the crisis.

First, in terms of the extent of the crisis, as already briefly mentioned, the three most affected countries have been Thailand, Indonesia and the Republic of Korea. *Malaysia* has also experienced a currency depreciation of 35 per cent and a fall in equity prices of 52 per cent, similar to that of Thailand, but the impact on the real economy has been more recent. A likely reason is that Malaysia had a significantly lower exposure to short-term foreign debt when the crisis broke. It has thus been less severely affected by the increased debt repayment and servicing burden caused by currency depreciation. But it does have one of the highest ratios of domestic bank lending to the private sector and this, in the context of the sharp fall in equity prices, has been a major factor behind its eventual slide into recession.

The *Philippines* also suffered a large currency depreciation and fall in share prices although its exposure to foreign short-term debt is even lower than that of Malaysia. The main impact of the financial crisis is being felt through the rise in interest rates that was introduced to shore up the peso. This has dampened investment and will slow down growth to 1 per cent in 1998 according to IMF forecasts, with which major international financial houses concur. Moreover, given that its pre-crisis growth rates were lower than those of other Asian countries (5.4 per cent in 1996) the adjustment burden will be somewhat milder.

Other Asian countries and areas, such as *China, Singapore, Viet Nam* and *Hong Kong, China*, have felt relatively milder effects from the crisis. Hong Kong, China, successfully defended its currency peg against the US dollar when that came under speculative attack in October 1997 but it did suffer a 20 per cent drop in share prices, and property prices have also fallen sharply. The higher interest rates and the adverse wealth effect will lead to a 3 per cent decline in GDP in 1998. The declared policy is to maintain the currency peg with the US dollar since, given the growing weight of high value-added services and manufactures in its production structure, Hong Kong, China, is not unduly concerned about the effects of the devaluation of regional currencies on its competitiveness.

The story is similar in *Singapore*. In spite of its strong fundamentals (huge foreign exchange and fiscal reserves, and a solid financial sector) Singapore was not entirely spared the contagion effects of the Asian crisis. Its currency depreciated by a moderate 15 per cent and the stock market fell by 13 per cent. Nevertheless, growth in 1997 remained at a high level of 7.8 per cent. This was explained by the fact that "a large part of Singapore's regional trade consists of intra-firm movements of parts, components and final products by multinational companies for export to end-markets in the OECD countries. As final demand from the United States and the European Union was healthy, Singapore's overall trade was not too seriously affected by the regional crisis".[1] However, growth forecasts for 1998 have been revised substantially downwards to 0.5 per cent. This is based on the fact that growth in the finance, tourism and transportation sectors, which have a strong regional orientation, has slowed down significantly because of the regional crisis.

China and *Viet Nam* have been relatively insulated from the currency and capital market turmoil in Asia by the fact that they have not undergone significant liberalization of the financial sector and have low foreign debt exposure. The main impact of the crisis will be felt through a slowing down of foreign direct investment (FDI) inflows from crisis-affected countries in the region that were important investors in these two countries. Export growth is also expected to slow down. In the case of Viet Nam, this is because 70 per cent of its exports go to South-East and East Asia. The depressed import demand in these latter countries will mean slower export growth in spite of the 15 per cent devaluation of the Vietnamese dong. In the case of China, the main impact will be felt through the loss of competitiveness as a result of the large devaluations of regional currencies, and a key question is whether it too will have to devalue in response. Due to these effects, GDP growth is forecast to decelerate significantly in these two countries. GDP growth in 1998 is forecast to be 4.0 and 5 per cent, respectively, in Viet Nam and China.

There were several channels through which the crisis spread to other Asian countries from those first affected. The first was through trade linkages. This is fairly significant given the fact that intra-regional trade accounts for 50 per cent of total international trade in Asia.[2] The sharp contraction in GDP and even more severe import compression in the worst-affected countries implies a corresponding fall in the export demand for other Asian countries. Export prospects for these other countries are also adversely affected by the loss of competitiveness as a result of the large currency devaluations in the worst-affected countries. Secondly, there have been growing financial linkages within the region. These have taken the form of foreign direct investment, bank lending and capital market activities.[3] These linkage effects imply that there is a vicious circle at work, with deepening recession in the worst-affected countries pulling other countries down and further weakening regional economic growth. Moreover, there also appears to have been an element of "pure contagion" effect at work, that is, the loss of international investor confidence unrelated to economic fundamentals. The extent to which this has occurred remains controversial. Those who argue that this has been large attribute it to the strong inherent imperfections in the global financial market.

1.3 ORIGINS AND NATURE OF THE CRISIS

A great deal has been written on the origins and nature of the crisis since its onset. Apart from understandable media interest there has also been a steady stream of analyses of the issue by academics, central bankers and policy-makers.[4] There are several reasons for this high degree of interest. One is the sheer unexpectedness and magnitude of the crisis that struck a set of countries long considered as "economic miracles".

Another is the ongoing apprehension over the potential spread of contagion effects beyond Asia to the rest of the world economy. Yet another is that, to many observers, there appeared to have been new and unprecedented elements of the crisis which did not fit standard models of currency and financial crises and which could not easily be understood by reference to recent experiences such as the Mexican crisis in 1995. Taking this view, some of these new elements, such as the sudden and massive shift in sentiments towards these countries on the part of international financial markets, the relative ineffectiveness of efforts so far to stabilize markets, and the general failure on the part of governments, international organizations and markets to anticipate the crisis, pose new and difficult problems for analysis. They also raise critical issues of national and international public policy in the context of growing globalization of financial markets.

Some economists have argued that none of the main elements of the crisis are new or unprecedented.[5] They point out that the bursting of asset bubbles (real estate and stock markets) has been a common feature in economic history. Similarly, the fact that there were no warning signals is also typical of financial crises. They see these features as manifestations of the severe imperfections that characterize financial markets. Foremost among these imperfections is that there is a large problem of asymmetric information in international lending wherein international lenders have limited and poor information about local borrowers. This leads lenders to over-extend credit, including to unsound local banks and companies. Perceptions that there are implicit guarantees by governments to maintain fixed exchange rates and to bail out local borrowers reinforce this process. At the same time, borrowers are also encouraged by the same perceptions with respect to fixedness of the exchange rate and government bail-outs. These market failures thus increase the riskiness of international lending and hence the vulnerability to periodic crises. In such a context it becomes a rational response for individual international lenders to follow the herd when danger signs of a crisis emerge. This "herding" phenomenon generates self-fulfilling panic that leads to large market overreactions that are not warranted by economic fundamentals.

To proponents of these arguments, the current Asian crisis, instead of constituting a new phenomenon, has in fact merely provided confirmation of their view of international financial markets. There had clearly been extremely rapid growth of foreign capital inflows in the past few years before the onset of the crisis. With hindsight, it is also clear that this was overdone, with prudential limits of risk accumulation being exceeded. There was also the uniform failure of credit-rating agencies and others to foresee the impending crisis. The spread on loans to the crisis-affected countries remained very low until the crisis broke. Most importantly, the swift and massive outflow of capital once the crisis broke in Thailand is seen as a classic illustration of self-fulfilling financial panic.

What is at least clear is that the crisis was caused by many factors and the conjunctural inter-reaction among them. It is thus unlikely that singling out one or two causes will yield an adequate explanation. Similarly, it will be difficult to assign weights to indicate the relative importance of different factors. The best that can be done at this stage is to highlight some of the factors that appear, to many observers, to be important parts of the explanation of the crisis.

"Crony" capitalism and the failure
of the Asian model

The basic divide in the debate over the causes of the crisis is between those who attribute blame to the malfunctioning of international financial markets and those who see domestic factors as the primary cause. For the latter, the crisis is best understood as the consequence of a defective Asian model of development that deviated from the principles of free market economics. Although the crisis-affected countries had pursued open economic policies and had pursued macroeconomic policies in line with the prescriptions of the "Washington Consensus" there were serious failings in other respects that turned out to have grave consequences. These failings have been encapsulated in the term "crony capitalism". A key element of this is widespread political interference with market processes. This covered several sins such as give-away privatizations to the relatives and cronies of the political leadership, the granting of artificial monopoly rights, government direction of credit towards political allies and government bail-outs of politically connected enterprises. These practices all amount to a supplanting of free and open competitive market processes by corrupt rent-seeking behaviour. A side effect of such a system is the creation of moral hazard in the form of expectations of government guarantees to politically connected lending. All this invariably resulted in a misallocation of investment, falling returns to investment and growing fragility in the financial system.[6] It will be noticed that this version of the failings of the Asian model focuses on corruption and the consequential lack of transparency in economic management. A related critique blames corruption but puts the stress on dirigiste policies *per se*. This relates to features of the Asian development model such the role of government in the selective promotion of industries and in the coordination of investment, and control over the allocation of credit and capital account transactions.[7] These deviations from laissez-faire are seen as having high costs in terms of reduced economic efficiency.

International capital markets

Those who argue that the crisis has largely been caused by the malfunctioning of international capital markets have strongly questioned the validity of this crony capitalism explanation. A basic counter-argument is that an adequate explanation for the crisis can be provided without the need to invoke crony capitalism. Similar currency and financial crises have occurred in countries which have been free of these presumed Asian vices.[8] A recent case in point was the financial crisis in Scandinavia in the early 1990s. A related counter-argument is that crony capitalism and dirigiste policies cannot constitute a sufficient explanation for the crisis.[9] One element of this is that while there is no denying the existence of corruption and cronyism in the crisis-affected Asian countries, it is no worse than in emerging market economies elsewhere. The rates of return on investment in South-East and East Asian economies were significantly higher than in other developing regions in the pre-crisis period, even after the decline observed in the immediate pre-crisis years. It is thus difficult to make the case that these were uniquely Asian weaknesses that led to the onset of the crisis. Another, and related, difficulty with the crony capitalism and over-interventionist explanation is the question of timing. In order for this to have been the cause of the crisis it is necessary to show that the extent of these failings has *increased* in the years leading up to the crisis. If these failings had always been present and compatible with high growth in the pre-crisis period, then it needs to be explained why, other things being equal, they should have provoked the crisis. In fact there is no clear evidence that there had been an increase in the extent of cronyism or interventionism in the years immediately prior to the crisis.

Recent work on the Republic of Korea has also challenged the empirical validity of the crony capitalism argument.[10] It has been argued that two key elements of the crony capitalism argument did not apply. First, it was untrue to say that there had been government guarantees to banks and corporations which created the problem of moral hazard with respect to foreign loans. Several large enterprises, including the tenth largest *chaebol* (conglomerate), had been allowed to go under in the immediate pre-crisis period. Second, contrary to the picture painted by the moral hazard story, most of the foreign borrowing went into the tradeable sector and not to fuel asset bubbles in the non-tradeable sector. As for the claim that over-interventionist policies were at the root of the crisis, it has been argued that inappropriate deregulation was a more plausible cause. This included the abandonment of investment coordination which led to over-capacity in several industries; the ending of rule-based state-business relationships which opened the way for less transparent relationships; and the failure to put in place adequate regulation of the newly liberalized financial sector.

In sum, the core of the case against the crony capitalism explanation is that there has been no rigorous proof that this has indeed been the main explanation. It smacks too much of wisdom after the fact, involving the identification of new sources of weaknesses in the Asian model that had been barely raised earlier. There is also the impression that much of the argument has been ideologically driven, seeking to make the point that the US version of capitalism is the only viable one nowadays.

Financial liberalization and fragility

The latter point links this debate on the causes of the Asian crisis to the larger debate that has been provoked on the desirability of intensifying financial globalization. The view that is being pushed by what critics have dubbed the "Wall Street Treasury complex" is that it is imperative for all countries to push ahead with capital account liberalization in order to reap the full benefits of globalization. The benefits from participating in financial globalization are depicted as being analogous to the benefits from free trade. "Free movement allocates capital to its most productive uses across countries and allows residents of different countries to engage in welfare-improving intertemporal consumption smoothing. In a competitive model with perfect foresight and complete markets, the welfare benefit from intertemporal trade is identical to the welfare benefit from international trade in goods and services."[11]

Opponents of this view of course dispute the depiction of international capital markets as being essentially the same as markets for goods and services.[12] As pointed out earlier, they see endemic problems of asymmetric information in international financial markets that lead to periodic crises. Taking this view, therefore, the putative benefits from capital account liberalization have to be set against the large economic and social costs of financial crises which countries with open capital accounts become vulnerable to. In this context it has been pointed out that the effects of financial crises can be not only devastating when they hit but also long-lasting in retarding growth.

The benefits of capital account liberalization have also been questioned. A recent study,[13] comparing the growth performance of countries that have liberalized capital accounts and those that have not, has found no evidence that the former group performed better. In addition, there have been many cases in recent economic history of countries having enjoyed high growth without liberalized capital accounts. This was true of Japan in the 1950s and 1960s, of the Republic of Korea until recently, and is true of China today. There are thus no proven benefits from capital account liberalization while, at the same time, there are significant examples of it not being essential for achieving high growth.

Another major difference between the opposing positions is over the extent to which domestic policies can protect countries with open capital accounts from the risk of financial crisis. Advocates of liberalization maintain that such good domestic policies as sound macroeconomic policies, adhering to transparent market-based policies and maintaining a well-regulated financial system can effectively ward off the risk of financial crisis. This would then permit the enjoyment of the benefits of liberalization without incurring any of the risks.

To critics, however, this is easier said than done. They point to several inherent difficulties in managing an economy with open capital accounts.[14] A basic one is that there are virtually no effective instruments for dealing with a large surge in capital inflows such as that which occurred in the past few years before the crisis in Asia. Short of reintroducing capital controls, the main instrument available is to sterilize part of the capital inflow. But this is costly and not sustainable for long. It is costly because it typically involves the selling of domestic bonds by the government (in order to acquire part of the inflow of foreign currency) on which a higher rate of interest has to be paid than the returns available on its holdings of foreign reserves. Bearing this cost of sterilization, in itself, creates problems of sustainability. In addition, however, sterilization will also prevent the differential between domestic and foreign interest rates from narrowing and hence will do little to reduce continued inflows of foreign capital. It will also raise domestic public debt that undermines policy credibility if sterilization is pursued for too long. Other forms of control through bank regulation and the raising of reserve requirements also have costs and cannot be pursued for too long before being circumvented. Such measures, of course, also go against the very logic of financial liberalization.

Critics of financial liberalization also point out that increased fragility in the financial system is a usual concomitant of financial liberalization and is difficult to prevent. One result of freeing entry into the financial sector is the lowering of the franchise value of banks and other financial institutions. This has the result of encouraging more risky behaviour on their part, since less is now at stake. Another factor making for greater financial fragility is that the social costs of increased foreign borrowing is not internalized by private borrowers, leading to excessive borrowing in the aggregate. These effects can, of course, be attenuated by stronger regulation of the newly liberalized financial system but this is often difficult to achieve quickly. The building-up of the necessary skills in risk management and loan management is a slow process involving an extended period of "learning by doing".

These inherent difficulties are of great significance to opponents of capital account liberalization since they also take the view that large surges of capital inflows are not a rare occurrence. The reason is that such surges reflect an unavoidable once-off adjustment. With good economic performance such as high growth and low inflation, governments and the private sector acquire an improved capacity to borrow internationally. When this is permitted by financial liberalization, "corporations and authorities alike then face higher borrowing ceilings. As they move from one level of external borrowing to a higher level, the resulting once-off stock effect translates into a sudden increase in capital flows. The surge is transitory in nature, which presents the recipient country with a severe trade-off."[15] Given the limited availability of effective policy instruments available for dealing with the surge of inflows, it is common for this to lead to increased financial fragility and other sources of vulnerability and then to a currency and financial crisis. This, together with the susceptibility of international financial markets to self-fulfilling panic at the first signs of trouble, makes "a sudden shift from boom to bust"[16] more likely than a gradual adjustment that ensures a "soft landing".[17]

Domestic policy failures

The foregoing debate has shown how difficult it is to arrive at a pat conclusion on what caused the crisis. There are clearly persuasive arguments on both sides but it would be wrong, in my view, to end on a purely agnostic note.

Let us concede that there was such a major malfunctioning of international capital markets such that crony capitalism alone is an insufficient cause of the crisis. Let us further concede that crony capitalism is not a uniquely Asian vice. In addition, let us also accept that the international financial system placed severe constraints on the scope for domestic policy. Does it then follow that we can entirely absolve domestic policy failures?

In my view, no, for two reasons: first, one cannot be morally neutral about crony capitalism. At heart, it involves corruption, the subversion of democracy and the rule of law, and social injustice. It is therefore deplorable in and of itself, irrespective of its role in provoking the crisis. Second, the existence of strong external constraints emanating from international financial markets does not make domestic policies immune from judgement. On the particular hazards of integration into global financial markets, it is apposite to recall that "that which is ineffectual in stopping a line of development altogether is not, on that account, altogether ineffectual. The rate of change is often of no less importance than the direction of change itself; but while the latter frequently does not depend upon our volition, it is the rate at which we allow change to take place which may well depend upon us. A belief in spontaneous progress must make us blind to the role of government in economic life. This role consists often in altering the rate of change, speeding it up or slowing it down as the case may be; if we believe that rate to be unalterable — or even worse, if we deem it a sacrilege to interfere with it — then, of course, no room is left for intervention."[18]

There can be little doubt that elements of crony capitalism played a role in provoking the crisis, even though not the predominant one some have ascribed to it. Especially in Indonesia, Malaysia and Thailand, connections between politicians in power and certain private enterprises created a moral hazard problem whereby these enterprises were seen as carrying an implicit guarantee against insolvency. There was thus a strong incentive for financial institutions to lend to these enterprises, regardless of the soundness of their operations. The moral hazard problem arose even more directly when banks and finance companies themselves had close political connections. In some cases these problems were made worse by direct political interference in the allocation of credit and in creating monopolies in certain activities. These types of political interference in the operation of markets are clearly likely to have contributed to the problem of excessive and misallocated investment and a consequent lowering of the rate of return on capital.

From the standpoint of overall development strategy it could also be argued that it was unwise to persist in pursuing exceptionally high growth through increasing reliance on foreign borrowing. Unlike the typical developing country, these Asian economies had exceptionally high rates of domestic saving of over 30 per cent of GDP. There was thus little need or justification to seek to augment these investable resources through foreign borrowing. Pushing up investment rates to 40 per cent or more through foreign borrowing could only contribute to a lowering of the rate of return from investment. As it turned out much of the excess investment (except in the case of the Republic of Korea) went into financing asset price inflation and the growth of non-tradeable activities with relatively low returns. It is also arguable that there were danger signals of overheating that were not acted upon. The abrupt rise in asset prices was a case in point. In addition, especially in Malaysia and Thailand, the sharply increased reliance on foreign workers over this period should have raised questions about the sustainability of the very high rates of growth.

There were also inadequacies in the handling of the impact of the huge surge in capital inflows in the years immediately preceding the crisis (see table 1.2). These inflows were very large, amounting up to 12.7 per cent of GDP in Thailand in 1995. Several features of the policy regimes supported these large inflows. The first was the policy of pegging exchange rates to the dollar in the case of Thailand and Malaysia. This signalled a guarantee against exchange rate loss which encouraged both domestic borrowers and foreign lenders to increase the flow of funds. The second was the creation of incentives to foreign borrowing by maintaining domestic interest rates that were significantly higher than the world market rate. While it can be argued that this was largely unavoidable, being in part the result of attempts to sterilize some of the capital inflow, this should have signalled the need to look for additional instruments to deal with the foreign capital inflow problem.

Another basic shortcoming was the failure to ensure that financial liberalization was accompanied by the development of a commensurate capacity to monitor and regulate the newly liberated financial system. There were several dimensions to this problem. One was an information

Table 1.2. Net capital flows (% of GDP)

	1983-88	1989-95	1991	1992	1993	1994	1995	1996	1997
Thailand									
Private	3.1	10.2	10.7	8.7	8.4	8.6	12.7	9.3	−10.7
Official	0.7		1.1	0.1	0.2	0.1	0.7	0.7	4.9
Indonesia									
Private	1.5	4.2	4.6	2.5	3.1	3.9	6.2	6.3	1.6
Official	2.4	0.8	1.1	1.1	0.9	0.1	−0.2	−0.7	1.0
Korea, Rep. of									
Private	−1.1	2.1	2.2	2.4	1.6	3.1	3.9	4.9	2.8
Official		−0.3	0.1	−0.2	−0.6	−0.1	−0.1	−0.1	−0.1
Malaysia									
Private	3.1	8.8	11.2	15.1	17.4	1.5	8.8	9.6	4.7
Official	0.3		0.4	−0.1	−0.6	0.2	−0.1	−0.1	−0.1
Philippines									
Private	−2.0	2.7	1.6	2	2.6	5	4.6	9.8	0.5
Official	2.4	2.0	3.3	1.9	2.3	0.8	1.4	0.2	0.8
Singapore									
Private	5.0	3.8	1.7	−2.7	9.4	2.5	1.3	−10.1	−5.5
Official									
China									
Private	1.2	2.5	1.7	−0.9	4.5	5.6	5.2	4.7	3.7
Official	0.3	0.5	0.3	0.8	0.9	0.4	0.3	0.2	−0.1

Source: IMF: *World Economic Outlook*, Interim Assessment, Dec. 1997.

gap. Financial liberalization meant the privatization and decentralization of foreign borrowing, although no adequate systems were put in place to monitor the extent of borrowing and its term structure. As a consequence, the growing problem of over-leveraged, unhedged, short-term borrowing was not perceived early enough (see table 1.3). This created, in turn, a policy "blind spot" which ruled out the consideration of pre-emptive countervailing action.

This was linked to the problem of inadequate regulation of the domestic operations of the banking system. Weaknesses in accounting systems and disclosure rules meant that there was a lack of transparency about the operations and soundness of banks. This was compounded by

Table 1.3 International claims by foreign banks, ($ billions)

		Total outstanding	Non-bank Sector	Non-bank/ Total (%)	Short-term Debt	Foreign reserves	Short-term reserve
1995	Thailand	92.18	12.56	13.63	60.56	36.95	1.64
	Indonesia	48.93	27.93	57.08	25.97	14.79	1.76
	Korea, Rep. of	83.26	17.91	21.51	47.63	32.71	1.46
	Malaysia	18.76	5.54	29.53	7.27	23.90	0.30
	Philippines	8.07	3.12	38.63	5.28	7.78	0.68
	Singapore	282.03	5.65	2.00	1.22	68.70	0.02
	Hong Kong, China	513.04	22.58	4.40	7.85	55.42	0.14
	China	67.06	16.10	24.00	34.40	76.04	0.45
1996	Thailand	99.27	14.13	14.23	58.33	38.65	1.51
	Indonesia	57.85	34.36	59.40	32.23	19.28	1.67
	Korea, Rep. of	109.15	24.07	22.06	54.66	34.07	1.60
	Malaysia	25.91	6.92	26.70	11.07	27.13	0.41
	Philippines	13.51	4.15	30.71	7.97	11.75	0.68
	Singapore	287.24	6.71	2.34	2.00	76.85	0.03
	Hong Kong, China	469.96	26.73	5.69	14.26	63.83	0.22
	China	79.75	17.88	22.42	38.09	107.68	0.35
1997	Thailand	79.62	12.02	15.09	43.74	26.89	1.63
	Indonesia	62.68	38.60	61.58	34.71	17.40	2.00
	Korea, Rep. of	104.07	25.39	24.40	59.65*	21.10	2.83
	Malaysia	29.05	6.45	22.22	10.21	22.61	0.45
	Philippines	16.43	6.33	38.53	8.45*	8.74	0.97
	Singapore	297.85	8.01	2.69	2.00*	71.29	0.03
	Hong Kong, China	467.50	21.33	4.56	15.02*	75.34	0.20
	China	89.88	18.11	20.15	43.81*	143.36	0.31
1998**	Thailand				33.68	27.96	1.20
	Indonesia				30.19	12.20	2.47
	Korea, Rep. of				28.19	60.00	0.47
	Malaysia				9.75	22.08	0.44
	Philippines				7.95	11.40	0.70
	Singapore				2.00	79.00	0.03
	Hong Kong, China				14.84	82.12	0.18
	China				48.63	130.70	0.37
1999**	Thailand				34.92	30.98	1.13
	Indonesia				31.39	14.70	2.14
	Korea, Rep. of				23.02	72.89	0.32
	Malaysia				10.10	22.38	0.45
	Philippines				8.25	11.10	0.74
	Singapore				2.10	84.00	0.03
	Hong Kong, China				14.79	82.94	0.18
	China				54.46	125.60	0.43

Note: * EIU estimate.   ** EIU forecast.

Source: Bank for International Settlements: *International Banking and Financial Market Developments*, Basle., May 1998; *The Economist* Intelligence Unit: Country Risk Service, 2nd and 3rd quarter, 1998.

weak prudential regulation of the banking system, especially with respect to capital adequacy requirements. A related problem was the weakness of the project evaluation capacity in banks in the face of increased competition to lend in the context of financial liberalization. This, together with the removal of controls over the allocation of credit, increased the probability of a flow of funds into the fuelling of asset bubbles. In addition there were parallel weaknesses in the non-bank corporate sector: a lack of transparency, the poor quality of governance and the maintenance of high debt-to-equity ratios. All these weaknesses created the preconditions for growing systemic fragility in the financial and non-bank corporate sectors. While it is true that sophisticated financial regulation is difficult to develop rapidly, the point still remains that this factor was not taken into account in deciding on the timing and pace of financial liberalization.

This set of policy lapses coalesced into a critical mass of economic fragility, which contributed to the massive loss of confidence in international financial markets when the seeds of doubt were first sowed with the onset of the Thai currency crisis. It also greatly compromised the ability of these economies to withstand the shock of the large-scale outflow of foreign capital. In particular, the weakness in the financial sector proved to have large negative macroeconomic effects.

1.4 ECONOMIC POLICIES
The economic policy response to the crisis so far has also been the subject of controversy. One issue is the appropriateness of the response prior to the conclusion of agreements with the IMF by the Republic of Korea, Indonesia and Thailand. It is argued that, especially in the case of Thailand, there was an attitude of denial to the impending crisis and that danger signals such as a large current account deficit and an asset price bubble were ignored. Similarly, when the crisis spread to Malaysia the initial focus was on attacking foreign scapegoats instead of dealing with the crisis. As discussed earlier, this formed a part of the deficiencies in domestic policy which contributed to the onset of the crisis.

The heart of the controversy, however, is over the policies that have been adopted in the worst-affected countries after the conclusion of agreements with the IMF. A common criticism of these programmes questions the need for the fiscal tightening that has been included in them. Critics have argued that, given the huge deflationary shock caused by the massive outflow of capital, fiscal tightening was a perverse response.[19] It was also unnecessary, in view of the low levels of government debt in these countries and the fact that the balance of payments deficits had not been caused by loose fiscal policy in the first place. Some critics have argued that what is required is stable or even expansionary fiscal and monetary policy. The underlying view is that this would bring about an early restoration of high growth that would soon ease the debt-servicing burden and minimize adverse effects on the domestic economy. Others have also recommended avoiding fiscal tightening on the grounds that it is necessary to allow room for an essential tightening of monetary policy in order to stabilize currencies. Against this the IMF has maintained that the recommended fiscal tightening has been slight (1.5 per cent of GDP in the case of Thailand) and is necessary to pay for the cost of restructuring the financial sector.[20] It has also stressed that it has adopted a flexible attitude to these fiscal targets and that they have indeed been loosened when the economic downturn proved to be more severe than anticipated. This has been most pronounced in Indonesia where a fiscal deficit of 8.5 per cent of GDP has been allowed for in the latest revision of the IMF conditions (August 1998).

A similar debate has emerged over the extent to which monetary policy should be tightened and interest rates raised. The IMF position is that a significant rise in interest rates is necessary in order to restore confidence in currencies which have suffered massive depreciations. While acknowledging that this will impact negatively on the large number of domestic firms with high debt, the IMF argues that it is a lesser evil than a failure to stabilize currencies. The reasoning behind this is that with large numbers of firms carrying high levels of foreign short-term debt in these countries, an easing of their debt burden through a recovery of the exchange rate will do more to minimize insolvency than the maintenance of low interest rates. Moreover, the rise in interest rates need only be temporary since it can be reversed once confidence is restored in the currency market.

Critics, however, point out that this prescription does not appear to have worked; the substantial rise in interest rates in Thailand and Indonesia has not so far had the desired effect of restoring confidence in their currencies, especially in Indonesia. The explanation proffered is that high interest rates are not sufficient to compensate for the perceived rise in credit risks on the part of lenders to these countries. They may, instead, exacerbate fears that the exchange rate will weaken even further if it is perceived that they are not sustainable.[21]

A basic reason is that the raising of interest rates strengthens the deflationary forces unleashed by the massive outflow of capital since the onset of the crisis. As mentioned earlier, given the many banks and other enterprises facing liquidity problems, a rise in interest rates can have a strong deflationary impact not only directly through its impact on illiquid enterprises but also through negative external effects on other enterprises. This can set off a vicious circle that pushes the economy into depression.

Another risk associated with the high interest rate policy is that there is no guarantee it will have its intended effect of restoring market confidence. Basically, little is known about what will be necessary to restore confidence in particular circumstances. "Confidence is an elusive concept. One is tempted to define it as a successful outcome, but then all we are left with is the unhelpful tautology that successful policies lead to successful outcomes ... The issue of how to restore confidence becomes even more complicated when we ask whose confidence? Often we think of 'the market', ignoring the fact that there are different groups — domestic investors, outside investors, speculators etc. — that have sys-tematically different information, initial portfolio compositions, and risk preferences. Steps like higher interest rates might restore the inflow of foreign capital, at the same time that it heightens uncertainty and increases the chances of a weaker economy, leading prudent domestic investors to diversify by moving their own money out of the country."[22]

From the earlier description of the crisis it does appear that "raising of interest rates did not restore confidence since exchange rates con-tinued to fall; and capital flight, from at least some of the countries, con-tinued."[23] The larger than expected decline in the real economy in all crisis-affected countries is also not inconsistent with the view that high interest rates can have strong deflationary effects when they fail to restore confidence relatively quickly.

Given the complex factors at work in the crisis, there is no way of conclusively establishing the correctness of one or the other view on the desirability of raising interest rates. In a deepening crisis, political leaders and policy-makers have often to act on their judgement of which view is correct or of what is in their best interests.

In this context the Malaysian decision at the beginning of September to cut loose from the IMF orthodoxy on high interest rates is of considerable interest. The decision involved the introduction of capital account controls accompanied by fixing the exchange rate and an easing of monetary policy. The aim is to halt the economic contraction which began in the first quarter of this year through easing the liquidity squeeze in the economy brought about by the capital outflow and depreciating exchange rates. The reason why capital controls had to be introduced was that an easing of monetary policy in the context of free capital mobility would result in a further depreciation of the exchange rate. This would add to the liquidity problems of the financial and corporate sectors and hence nullify the effects of an easing of monetary policy. "A basic principle of open macroeconomics is that we can only have two of the three following features: a fixed exchange rate, full capital mobility and monetary policy independence. Any pair is possible but any attempt at achieving all three inevitably results in a currency crisis."[24] The Malaysian move can thus be understood as giving up capital mobility in order to regain *both* monetary independence and a fixed exchange rate.

At the time of writing (early September) it is of course too early to tell what effect this policy shift will have. But it will certainly be watched with considerable interest, especially by other crisis-affected countries in the region. What is unfolding is a real-world experiment with an alternative set of policies to those which, so far, do not seem to have succeeded in stemming the crisis.

The underlying rationale for the move is that the exchange rate, like those of other crisis-affected countries, has remained undervalued for too long and this has not been reversed by high interest rates. This has provoked deep recession that is destroying even viable and well-managed enterprises and inflicting high social costs. The new measures seek to break this vicious circle by stabilizing the exchange rate at a more appropriate level and by lowering interest rates to allow the financial and corporate sectors to deleverage and restructure. The hope is that this will restore confidence within the domestic economy and lead to recovery in economic activity.

Sceptics have made the point that the new policies are unlikely to be sustainable for very long. The reason is that capital controls will increasingly be circumvented and the cost of distortions created by this will grow over time. It will, nevertheless, provide a window of opportunity. But this needs to be used wisely. If it is used to avoid or delay such necessary reforms as the restructuring of the financial and corporate sectors, then it will only succeed in postponing the evil day. When capital controls are inevitably removed or relaxed, then the prediction is for a sharp fall in the exchange rate and renewed crisis. If, in contrast, the opportunity is used to undertake the restructuring necessary, then the experiment could work, since the economy would be reopening itself to international capital markets with strengthened fundamentals.

For those who see the origins of the crisis in the panic reactions of the international capital market, the relevant test is whether the Malaysian experiment succeeds in stabilizing the economy and, beyond that, whether the economy can restore growth without returning to free capital mobility. In this sense it provides a test of the two opposing views on the desirability of proceeding with the push for free capital mobility in the current phase of globalization. A critical test of the Malaysian experiment is therefore whether the economy can continue to attract foreign direct investment while maintaining controls over volatile short-term capital flows. Past economic growth in Malaysia had in fact been heavily dependent on foreign direct investment. Indeed, the announced policy change was careful to emphasize that "Malaysia has not turned away from all forms of foreign capital. Free flows of foreign direct investment and repatriation of interest, profits, dividends and capital continue to be guaranteed. Current account transactions remain generally convertible."[25] In principle, there is no reason why foreign direct investment should shun Malaysia if it remains an attractive production site. After all, there have been large recent inflows of foreign direct investment into countries without free capital mobility such as China and Viet Nam. It is also relevant to note that the new controls will only bring the Malaysian currency in line with the restrictions prevailing over the Philippine peso, the Korean won, and the New Taiwan dollar.[26] Moreover, it could be argued that with its very high rates of domestic investment (of over 30 per cent of GDP) Malaysia has little need to rely on short-term foreign capital to raise the rate of investment. Indeed, the high domestic saving and investment rate means that the marginal returns from additional investment funded from foreign borrowing are bound to be low.

Whatever the outcome of this Malaysian experiment, it is relevant to note that other proposals have been made for stabilizing currencies in the region. Notably, the case has been made that joint regional action is required to stabilize the situation.[27] The starting-point for this argument is that the currencies of the crisis-affected countries remain seriously undervalued and need to be nudged upwards to moderate the macroeconomic havoc that this is causing. But "because of the domino effects of the dollar devaluations in the East Asian region the problem is a collective one. If exchange appreciation is tried in just one country, it would lack credibility when the currencies of its industrial competitors remained undervalued. Thus, to begin nudging all currencies upward simultaneously requires regional coordination."[28]

The last major area of controversy is over the structural reforms that have been prominently embedded in the agreements with the IMF. These involve the immediate problem of restructuring or closure of insolvent banks and other financial institutions, as well as institutional reforms such as strengthening regulation of the financial sector, instituting effective bankruptcy laws, increasing the transparency of corporate governance, and liberalizing laws limiting foreign ownership in the corporate and financial sectors of the economy. These structural reforms are seen by the IMF to be critical requirements for the restoration of international market confidence in these economies and hence for their recovery.

There have been two main strands of criticism to this approach. The first has questioned the wisdom of making these structural reforms an integral part of what should have essentially been stabilization packages. Some have argued that the focus should have concentrated on life-saving core economic issues rather than diluting it by introducing inherently difficult and time-consuming issues of institutional reform. While not questioning the need for such reforms, they stress that the timing is inappropriate. This is joined to a related political economy argument that by front-loading difficult reforms within the policy package the IMF may have pushed the process beyond an optimal level of conditionality. Given the political fragility in some of these countries, such a tough reform line may ultimately prove counter-productive since it is beyond the capacity of governments to implement.

The second strand of criticism of these structural reform measures springs in large part from nationalist and populist sentiment. A major grievance concerns the liberalization of laws relating to foreign ownership in the financial and corporate sectors. This is seen as an exploitation of the current weaknesses of these countries by major powers, a perception that is heightened by the fact that equity prices have collapsed dramatically in the wake of the crisis. The latter implies that foreign purchases of national assets are being made at distress prices and hence unfair. The upshot would be a loss of national ownership and control over key sectors of the economy that would reduce future policy autonomy.

A key consideration in evaluating this second strand of criticism is a judgement on the extent to which current asset prices reflect the fundamental worth of companies in distress.[29] While there was certainly overvaluation until the crisis, there are also grounds for thinking that the overreaction in currency and equity markets referred to earlier makes this a bad time to sell. At the same time, however, it must be recognized that this may be the only alternative to going under. The choice may simply be either accepting more foreign ownership or losing the enterprise altogether to the national economy. Besides, an increased inflow of foreign direct investment will contribute to overcoming the crisis by injecting badly needed capital as well as the technology and managerial skills necessary to strengthen the corporate and financial sectors. But, in order to realize the latter benefits, it will be important to promote sales to foreign buyers that really are more efficient than alternative local investors.

There is no simple way of resolving this debate. A fundamental problem is that of the counterfactual. The potential effects of alternative policies advocated by critics cannot be verified until they are actually applied in the current crisis situation. They may have equally strong analytical arguments in their favour as the policies that are currently being pursued, but the issue cannot therefore be confidently resolved on *a priori* grounds.

This is not to say that arguments for alternative policies should be ignored. They constitute, as it were, "shadow policies" which could be seriously considered should parts of current policies fail to yield their anticipated results. In situations where professional opinion is seriously divided and where there is a high degree of uncertainty, as is the case in the current situation, a greater than usual degree of flexibility in policy implementation would be in order. Close monitoring of the unfolding effects of current policies and a willingness to change course when warranted would clearly be desirable. And, in that monitoring, the impact of policies on the level of unemployment and social costs should be a prominent consideration. In particular, at least temporarily increased social spending may be unavoidable if countries are to undertake credible efforts to alleviate the gravest social consequences of the crisis.

1.5 OUTLOOK

It is clear that 1998 will be a bad year but it is far more difficult to forecast how soon and how strongly the recovery will come. An initial optimistic view was that the crisis would be "V-shaped" in nature, that is, a deep and sharp recession followed by an equally steep recovery, as was the case of the recent Mexican crisis. However, this has clearly not materialized.

A basic reason is that the key to rapid recovery is the restoration of confidence in these countries in international financial markets, but the requirements for achieving this are quite formidable. They extend beyond conventional stabilization measures, such as the reduction in current account deficits, to difficult challenges of financial sector reform and corporate sector restructuring. Apart from the immediate problem of reducing current fragility in the banking system, which will itself be a costly exercise for government budgets, credible steps to correct the deficiencies in financial sector regulation will also need to be taken simultaneously. This is because the loss of confidence in these economies was provoked not only by the immediate debt problems but also by a perception, albeit belated, of systemic fragility in the financial sector. Deep reform of the financial sector is inherently difficult and time-consuming and also involves overcoming political vested interests. A degree of uncertainty therefore remains as to whether firm initial measures that are credible enough to financial markets will be implemented.

Similar observations apply to the problem of corporate workouts and restructuring. There is the immediate and difficult problem of performing a "triage" to save viable enterprises through orderly workouts. But there is also the need for simultaneous action to correct deficiencies in corporate governance, such as the lack of transparency and poor accounting systems. Particular attention will need to be paid to the issue of reducing the typically high debt-to-equity ratios and imprudent reliance on short-term foreign borrowing. As in the case of financial sector reform, a critical issue is whether credible signals on the seriousness of the reform effort can quickly be sent to financial markets.

It should, of course, be noted that these reform efforts are necessary not only for restoring confidence to international financial markets but are also essential, in themselves, for economic recovery. Delayed or half-hearted reform efforts will only perpetuate fragility in the financial and corporate sectors and impede recovery. In particular, without a swift restoration of confidence in the banking system and normal functions of financial intermediation, the potential recovery in exports permitted by the currency devaluations will remain underexploited.

Other sources of uncertainty over the prospects for recovery remain. One is the question of whether an export-led recovery will be able to play its full role. On the positive side, the recovery in the European Union and continued steady growth in the United States provide favourable prospects for export growth, unless they trigger pro-tectionist responses. But this must be set against the continuing uncer-tainty over the prospects for reflationary measures in Japan, the possibility of competitive devaluations of other currencies in the region and mounting contagion effects beyond the region. The growing risk of social unrest and political instability in some of the most severely affected countries also must be recognized.

Taking all the above considerations into account, it would appear that an immediate bounce back is highly unlikely. Indeed most forecasts predict, at best, the beginnings of a moderate recovery in the second half of 1999. Whether or not growth will, thereafter, return to the heady levels of the pre-crisis period must for the moment remain an open question.

Finally, it is important to note that there are significant differences in the recovery prospects for the three most severely affected countries. This is directly related to the extent to which they have embarked upon and are pursuing credible reform measures. The Republic of Korea and Thailand appear to be on track for recovery, whereas considerable uncertainty remains over the prospects for Indonesia.

Notes and references

[1] Singapore Government: *1998 Budget Statement*, issued on 31 March 1998.

[2] Corbett and Vines, 1998, p 3.

[3] Park and Song, 1998.

[4] See, for example, Condon, 1998a; Grenville, 1997, 1998a; Krugman, 1998b; Macfarlane, 1997; Sachs, 1997, 1998; Stiglitz, 1997, 1998d, 1998e; and Bibliography.

[5] See in particular Wyplosz, 1998, and Stiglitz, 1998a, 1998b.

[6] Krugman, 1998a, 1998c.

[7] Greenspan, 1998a, 1998b.

[8] Wyplosz, 1998.

[9] Stiglitz, 1998a, 1998b.

[10] Chang, 1998, and Chang, Park and Yoo, 1998.

[11] Dooley, 1998, p. 85.

[12] Bhagwati, 1998.

[13] Rodrik, 1998.

[14] Calvo, Leiderman and Reinhart, 1996.

[15] Wyplosz, 1998, p. 7.

[16] ibid, p. 8.

[17] ibid, p. 8.

[18] Polanyi, 1957, pp. 36-37.

[19] See in particular Sachs and Radlets, 1998.

[20] Fischer, 1998a, 1998b.

[21] Grenville, 1998b.

[22] Stiglitz, 1998b, p. 20.

[23] ibid, p. 21.

[24] Wyplosz, 1998, p. 4.

[25] See Condon, 1998b.

[26] ibid.

[27] McKinnon, 1998a, 1998b.

[28] McKinnon, 1998a, p. 3.

[29] Krugman, 1998d.

THE SOCIAL IMPACT

2

2.1 INTRODUCTION

The economic slump provoked by the financial crisis has by now caused widespread social distress in the three worst-affected countries (Indonesia, Thailand and the Republic of Korea). A fall in output and incomes of the severity described in the previous chapter is invariably accompanied by massive job losses as bankruptcies and cutbacks in production multiply. This leads to a sharp rise both in open unemployment and underemployment. In addition, the rise in inflation, in the context of a considerably weakened labour market, extracts a further toll in terms of falling real wages and incomes. The combined effects of higher unemployment and inflation push large numbers of people into poverty.

Adverse developments of this magnitude constitute, in themselves, a substantial shock to any social system. But these effects are amplified in the three worst-affected countries by two additional features of their economic systems. The first is the absence of a meaningful social safety net. Of the three countries, only the Republic of Korea has an unemployment insurance system, but it is of recent origin and still of limited coverage and duration. Systems of social assistance are also rudimentary and are limited to persons who are incapable of work. The vast majority of displaced workers will thus have to fend for themselves during the crisis. The second feature lies in the fact that social expectations in these three coun-

Table 2.1. Principal characteristics of employment, 1996

	Total labour force	Unemployment rate (%)	Distribution by sector (%)			Distribution by occupational status (%) [1]		
			Agriculture	Industry	Services	Family workers	Self-employed	Employees
Indonesia	90.1	4.9	44	13.4	42.6	26.0	43.0	28.6
Thailand	32.4	1.5	40.4	16.7	42.9	19.7	31.0	40.1
Rep. of Korea	21.2	2.0	10.6	20.7	68.7	10.5	27.6	59.2
Malaysia	8.6	2.6	16.8	27.5	55.7	7.5	21.1	71.4
Hong Kong, China	3.1	2.8	0.3	15.9	83.8	0.8	10.3	86.9
Singapore	1.8	2.0	0.2	23.3	76.5	0.9	12.3	84.1

[1] Employment shares by occupation may add up to less than 100 for lack of information about the status of some workers.

Sources: World Bank: *World Development Indicators 1998*; ILO: *Yearbook of Labour Statistics 1997*; Asian Development Bank, Country Data, available on Website: http://internotes.asiandevbank.org/notes/edr0004p/Excel.htm.

tries have been shaped by a long period of increasing employment opportunities and this makes the current shock in the labour market all the ruder. Indeed, this combination of sharp and unexpected social pain on the one hand, and the lack of collectively provided relief on the other, is fertile ground for breeding social unrest.

It is important to discuss the pre-crisis labour market situation in South-East and East Asia as a prelude to examining the recent rise in unemployment and poverty. This is for two reasons. First, the full significance of the impact of the crisis on unemployment can only be appreciated in relation to past employment performance. Second, there are significant differences in employment structure among the six countries shown in table 2.1 which illustrate some of the difficulties involved in arriving at precise estimates of the rise in unemployment and underemployment.

A key characteristic is that, with the exception of Indonesia, all the countries shown in table 2.1 had enjoyed full employment over a sustained period of at least two decades. In 1996, the year before the crisis, rates of open unemployment in Thailand, the Republic of Korea, Malaysia, Singapore and Hong Kong, China, ranged from 1.5 to 2.8 per cent. Such low rates of open unemployment have rarely been seen anywhere else in the world since the early 1970s. This enviable employment performance was a direct consequence of the high rates of GDP growth that were sustained for over two decades before the crisis. The reliance on exports of labour-intensive manufactured products as the centrepiece of the growth strategy also contributed to high rates of employment growth.

The main engine of employment growth was the modern sector, consisting chiefly of manufacturing, construction and a variety of service activities. This rapid employment growth in the modern sector presented steadily expanding opportunities for peasants, agricultural labourers and those engaged in low-productivity informal sector activities to move into more productive and better-paid jobs. Although adverse international publicity about the quality of these modern-sector jobs may cast doubt on this depiction of the process, it nevertheless remains true that wages and benefits in the modern sector were far superior to those available in the rural and informal sectors. In fact, this growing absorption of labour into higher productivity modern-sector activities was the main mechanism through which the benefits of rapid economic growth were distributed to workers. A clear indicator of this was the significant decline in levels of poverty during the period of high growth in all countries shown in table 2.1. It is also relevant to note that in all these countries real wages increased after the exhaustion of the initial pool of surplus labour. Even in Indonesia, which still has the highest share of rural and informal sector employment, real wages were increasing at a rate of 4 to 6 per cent per annum by the 1990s.[1]

Another noteworthy feature of the growth and employment performance in all these countries was the previous absence of serious recessions or economic crises. High growth was only rarely interrupted and even then the recessions were shallow and short-lived. As a result, cyclical unemployment was virtually unknown and employment growth was on a constant rising trend. This benign employment situation is perhaps a major reason why no attempts were made to introduce unemployment insurance in any of these countries until the Republic of Korea did so in 1995.

Although the essential features of employment growth described above are common to these six countries, there are nevertheless substantial differences in the current structure of employment. The main reason for this is that the growth process started considerably earlier in Singapore, the Republic of Korea and Hong Kong, China, than in the other three countries and their initial income levels were also higher. These early starters have now joined the advanced countries in terms of per capita income and employment structure. Moreover, Singapore and Hong Kong, China, are city states and have never had any agricultural employment to speak of.

The main difference to note in the structure of employment in these six countries is that both Indonesia and Thailand still have respectively 44 and 40 per cent of total employment in agriculture, considerably higher than in the other four countries. Conversely, of course, employment in industry and services is much lower. Since agricultural employment consists predominantly of family-based work, this leads to another important difference: wage employment accounts for less than 30 per cent of total employment in Indonesia and the corresponding figure for Thailand is 40 per cent. The share of wage employment in total employment is, in fact, a fairly good indicator of the relative size of the modern sector in a developing economy. In contrast to the other four countries, traditional agriculture and the urban informal sector employment still employ significantly more than half of the labour force in Indonesia and Thailand.

Another noteworthy difference is the enormous variation in the size of the labour force among these six countries, ranging from less than 2 million in Singapore to 90 million in Indonesia. This needs to be borne in mind when interpreting aggregated figures on the impact of the crisis on unemployment. While good journalistic copy, such aggregates are misleading in view of these widely varying ranges in the size of the labour force.

2.2 THE UNEMPLOYMENT CRISIS

Table 2.2 summarizes the latest information available on the impact of the economic crisis on unemployment. A striking fact is, of course, the paucity of firm data (see second panel of table 2.2). Only the Republic of Korea and Hong Kong, China, have recent data on unemployment based on monthly labour force surveys. For Thailand, the only data available are from the May 1998 round of its thrice-yearly labour force survey and there are no recent data available for Indonesia and Malaysia.

What can be gleaned from the recent available data for these countries is the sharp rise that has occurred in open unemployment. Unemployment rates have doubled in Thailand and Hong Kong, China, and have increased more than threefold in the Republic of Korea between the onset of the crisis and circa mid-1998. This, in itself, is a huge shock to the labour market but the dislocation is even greater when the swiftness of the downturn in employment is taken into account. In the Republic of Korea and Hong Kong, China, most of the increase in unemployment has occurred in the first seven months of this year and is still continuing. In Thailand, partial information on job losses also indicate that there was an abrupt onset of rapid job loss from the third quarter of 1998.

Table 2.2. The increase in unemployment, 1997-98

	Pre-crisis		Latest available data			Estimates and forecasts for end 1998			
	Unemployment ('000)	Unemployment rate (%)	No. unemployed ('000)	Absolute increase ('000)	Unemployment rate (%)	No. unemployed ('000)	Absolute increase since crisis	Unemployment rate (%)	Retrenchments/Job losers ('000)
Indonesia	4 300 (Aug. '97)	4.9	n.a.	n.a.	n.a.	9 300 to 13 700	5 000 to 9 400	7.2 to 14.8	3 800 to 5 400
Thailand	698 (Feb. '97)	2.2	1 613 (May '98)	915	5.0	1 987	1 289	6.0	n.a.
Rep. of Korea	451 (Oct. '97)	2.3	1 651 (July '98)	1 200	8.2	n.a.	n.a.	n.a.	1 525 (stock at July '98)
Malaysia	224 (end '97)	2.6	n.a.	n.a.	n.a.	405	181	5.2	61 (Jan. to Sep. 1998) [cumulative]
Hong Kong, China	77	2.4	149	72	4.5	152	75	4.6	n.a.

n.a. = not available.

Sources: 1. ILO/UNDP: *Employment challenges of the Indonesian economic crisis* (Jakarta, June 1998). 2. Warburg Dillon Read: *Asian Adviser: August 1998*; 3. Republic of Korea, National Statistics Office, available on Website: http://www.nso.go/kr/report/data/ssec9807.htm; 4. Thailand, National Statistical Office: *Labour Force Surveys*.

The monthly employment data for the Republic of Korea illustrate the swift dynamics involved (table 2.3). The seasonally adjusted unemployment rate doubled in the four months between October 1997 and February 1998. By July 1998 it had increased by a further 74 per cent. The increase in the number of unemployed over this period was 1.2 million or 5.6 per cent of the total employment figure in November 1997. This suggests that about one in 20 workers lost their jobs over a period of only nine months.

There are also indications that the adverse impact on the labour markets of these countries has been more widespread than what is shown by the unemployment figures alone. Apart from open unemployment, the number of discouraged workers also seems to have increased. In the Republic of Korea the labour force participation rate fell from 63.1 per cent to 61.5 per cent between the second quarters of 1997 and 1998 (table 2.3). This represents a decrease in labour force participation of 1.6 million workers compared with what it would have been had the pre-crisis trend in labour force growth continued. It will be recalled that this is almost equivalent to the total number of the unemployed in July 1998. This suggests that a wider measure of unemployment would show a substantially higher level of labour market slack than that indicated by the standard unemployment rate. In Thailand the number of those of working age shown as being "not in the labour force" increased by 600,000 between the February rounds of the labour force surveys of 1997 and 1998. This is equivalent to a third of the number of unemployed in May 1998.

Earlier paragraphs in this section contained about all there is to be said on the impact of the crisis on the employed based on actual figures. But the importance of the issue, and the understandable interest in knowing more, has provoked national government agencies and international organizations to produce indirect estimates of a rise in unemployment and forecasts of how it will evolve. These estimates and forecasts are presented in the third panel of Table 2.2. For Thailand, the forecast (by the IMF) is for the unemployment rate to rise a further percentage point to 6 per cent by the end of 1998. In Malaysia the corresponding figure is 5.2 per cent, which would represent a doubling of the

Table 2.3. Republic of Korea employment trends (thousands)

	Economically active population (participation rate)	Employment	Variation over the previous period	Unemployment	Variation over the previous period	Unemployment rate (seasonally adjusted)
1996	21 188 (62.0)	20 764		425		2.0
First quarter 1997	21 112 (61.1)	20 466	−298	646	221	3.1 (2.6)
Second quarter 1997	21 868 (63.1)	21 319	853	550	−96	2.5 (2.6)
Third quarter 1997	21 806 (62.6)	21 336	17	470	−80	2.2 (2.4)
October 1997	21 793 (62.5)	21 341	5	451	−19	2.1 (2.3)
November 1997	21 762 (62.3)	21 188	−153	574	123	2.6 (2.9)
December 1997	21 340 (61.0)	20 682	−506	658	84	3.1 (3.1)
January 1998	20 645 (58.9)	19 711	−971	934	276	4.5 (4.1)
February 1998	20 760 (59.2)	19 562	−149	1 235	301	5.9 (4.7)
March 1998	21 270 (60.6)	19 982	420	1 378	143	6.5 (5.3)
April 1998	21 561 (61.3)	20 127	145	1 434	56	6.7 (6.1)
May 1998	21 717 (61.7)	20 226	99	1 492	58	6.9 (7.0)
June 1998	21 712 (61.6)	20 183	−43	1 539	47	7.0 (7.7)
July 1998	21 650 (61.4)	19 999	−184	1 651	112	7.6 (8.2)

Source: National Statistics Office, available on Website: http://www.nso.go/kr/report/data/ssec9807.htm.

pre-crisis level of unemployment. It would also represent a very rapid rate of increase of unemployment, as the recession in Malaysia began only in the first quarter of this year. Given the presence of a very large number of illegal foreign workers in this country, the Malaysian forecast may be an underestimate of the true extent of job loss. The job losses of illegal workers are unlikely to be captured in official statistics and therefore would not enter into calculations of the unemployment rate. The large presence of foreign workers will in fact act as a buffer, moderating the impact of the economic downturn for Malaysian workers. Latest available figures on retrenchments show that only 57,000 local workers have been affected between January and August 1998 and the Minister of Labour has stated that 80 per cent of these have been re-employed.[2]

The really dramatic forecasts are for Indonesia where, it will be recalled, GDP is forecast to fall by 15 per cent this year. The normal expectation is that this would translate into a staggering increase in the unemployment rate. Yet, as will be seen from table 2.2, there is no unanimity of views on this subject. Forecasts of the unemployment rate range widely from 7.2 to 14.8 per cent at the end of 1998. This vast difference does not arise from sharply divergent estimates of job losses resulting from the economic contraction (estimates which range from 3.8 to 5.4 million). Rather, it is linked to widely differing assumptions about the proportion of displaced workers that will be absorbed into informal sector employment (table 2.4). The low estimate of 7.2 per cent unemployment assumes that 48 per cent of displaced workers will find employment in the informal sector, whereas the high estimate assumes that all displaced workers will remain unemployed.

This difference between alternative forecasts of Indonesian unemployment brings us back to the issue of how differences in the structure of employment actually condition the adequacy of the unemployment rate as an indicator of distress in the labour market. In the introduction to this chapter it was pointed out that Indonesia still had about two-thirds of its total employment in the agricultural and informal sectors. It is thus a country where the labour market adjustment typical of low-income countries (whereby any emerging problem of open unemployment is solved by the absorption of the unemployed into the informal

Table 2.4. Indonesia: Alternative estimates of workers displaced by crisis (1998)

Sector	Total employment ('000)			Displaced workers in 1998			
				Estimate A		Estimate B	
	1996	1997	1998	All workers ('000)	As a percentage of employment	Wage workers ('000)	As a percentage of wage employment
Manufacturing	10 773	11 215	10 900	315	2.8	1 333	21.0
Construction	3 796	4 200	3 165	1 035	24.6	1 031	30.0
Trade/Hotels	16 103	17 221	14 341	2 880	16.7	546	21.0
Transport	3 943	4 138	3 343	795	19.2	323	21.0
Finance	690	657	492	165	25.1	185	30.0
Services/Other sectors	11 739	12 641	12 056	585	4.6	1 995	21.0
Whole economy	85 702	87 050	81 275	5 775	6.6	5 413	18.0

Estimate A is based on sectoral employment elasticities estimated by BAPPENAS, and assumes a 15% contraction in real GDP.   Estimate B is the ILO/UNDP estimate (June 1998). It uses sectoral employment elasticities for wage employment only and assumes 30% contractions in all sectors except agriculture, mining and utilities (where no labour displacement is assumed).

Source: Employment figures for 1996 and 1997 are drawn from BAPPENAS (Indonesian National Planning Agency), reported in ILO/UNDP: *Employment challenges of the Indonesian economic crisis* (ILO, Jakarta, June 1998).

sector) is most likely to apply. This adjustment mechanism involves both reverse migration to rural areas and entry into informal employment in urban areas. This process is driven by the desperation of the unemployed, in the absence of unemployment benefits or other social support, to seek any income-generating activity available, however derisory the income may be. At the same time, it is supposed to be facilitated by the family ties that urban workers retain with their rural areas as well as by the ease of entry into informal sector activities.

The issue is thus an empirical one of the extent to which this standard labour market mechanism is operating in Indonesia during the current crisis. There are several reasons for thinking that the assumption that half of the displaced workers will be absorbed in alternative employment is too optimistic. The first is the sheer magnitude of the problem. Given the anticipated drastic fall in output, there is little cause to disagree with the projected figure of job losses of 4 to 5 million workers, equivalent to about 8 per cent of the current total employment in the agricultural and informal sectors of the economy. To this we must add the bulk of the 2.8 million new entrants into the labour force, who will have to seek informal sector employment owing to the collapse of the modern sector. Furthermore, there was a backlog from 1997 of about 5 million unemployed, many of whom are also seeking informal sector or agricultural employment. The informal sector would thus need to absorb at least an additional 10 per cent of workers if the rate of open unemployment is to be contained at around 7 per cent. If we juxtapose the sheer magnitude of this labour absorption problem with the fact that the collapse in output will also mean a drastic fall in the demand for the goods and services produced by the informal sector, there would appear to be few grounds for optimism. A further consideration is that the traditional institutions facilitating labour absorption in rural areas have been eroded. Commercialization of agricultural production has reduced the role of family-based farms and many urban workers have gradually lost the necessary links to the rural areas to enable them to be reabsorbed there.

The really important issue, however, is not what the open unemployment rate will turn out to be by the end of the year. Rather, it is the overall welfare significance of the impact of the crisis on the labour market. The essential fact to be underscored is that by the end of the year the social costs of unemployment will have reached a very high level in Indonesia. First, the progress achieved through the growth of modern-sector employment will have been shattered. About a fifth of these jobs will be lost, along with the hopes of a better life for 4 to 5 million workers and their families. This will remain true regardless of what proportion of them find alternative employment in the traditional sector, since such employment represents a significant change for the worse. The material deprivation and psychological costs of all this on those severely affected must also be very high. Second, new entrants to the labour market face the bleakest of prospects of obtaining a job. Third, the collapse in output and consumption, together with high inflation, will mean sharp falls in real wages and earnings in both the formal and informal sectors.

2.3 THE RISE IN POVERTY

An employment crisis of the magnitude described earlier is bound to lead to a corresponding increase in poverty. This is so because, apart from Korea, the most severely affected countries have neither a system of unemployment benefits nor an adequate level of social assistance. For low-paid workers especially, the loss of employment means a fall into poverty unless there are other sources of income, such as the earnings of other members of the nuclear family or support from the extended family and community. These traditional welfare mechanisms have been weakened in the course of economic growth and modernization and are unlikely to save more than a tiny minority from poverty. In addition, the generalized economic hardship also means that the capacity to engage in such traditional redistribution is greatly diminished, even if the will to do so is still extant.

Apart from unemployment, the other major factor behind rising poverty is the fall in wages and incomes. Average earnings in the informal sector, already low to begin with, will be depressed further by the huge influx of new workers and declining demand for the goods and services produced by the sector. High inflation will also erode these informal-sector earnings as well as the wages of all workers. Wages are unlikely to be protected against inflation because of the weakened bargaining position of labour in the current depressed economic conditions. Those with wages and incomes that are not far above the poverty line will be easily pushed below it by this process.

An estimate of the likely increase in poverty in Indonesia, Thailand, and the Republic of Korea by the end of the year is presented in table 2.5, showing that an additional 20 per cent of the population will fall into poverty as a result of the crisis. Even in the Republic of Korea, the most economically advanced of these three countries, an additional 12 per cent of the population will become poor. The projected increase in Thailand is the same as in the Republic of Korea.

It is interesting to note from table 2.5 that the major cause of the increase in poverty in Indonesia is high inflation whereas in the other two countries it is the rise in unemployment. The simple explanation for this is the much higher rate of projected inflation in Indonesia in 1998 – 60 per cent as compared to 8 and 10 per cent respectively in the Republic of Korea and Thailand. The impact of inflation can be gauged from the fact that in Indonesia "the purchasing power of the minimum wage, unchanged between January 1997 and June 1998, ... could only purchase 2.6 kg of rice in mid-June 1998 compared with 6.3 kg a year and a half ago."[3]

These poverty estimates provide a telling summary of how widespread the negative social impact of the financial crisis has been and

Table 2.5. Increase in poverty due to crisis (1998 forecasts)

Country	Increase in the number of poor		Due to unemployment		Due to inflation	
	Millions	Percentage of population	Millions	Percentage of total increase	Millions	Percentage of total increase
Indonesia	39.9	20	12.3	30.8	27.6	69.2
Rep. of Korea	5.5	12	4.7	85.5	0.8	14.5
Thailand	6.7	12	5.4	80.6	1.3	19.4

Source: IMF: *World Economic Outlook*, October 1998.

will continue to be in the coming months. Between 10 to 20 per cent of the entire population of the worst-affected countries will fall into poverty, a dramatic reversal of the trend of rapid poverty-reduction in the pre-crisis period. This is over and above the undoubted further deterioration in the situation of those already in poverty before the onset of the crisis.

2.4 CONCOMITANT SOCIAL ILLS

In all probability, a host of social ills will be aggravated by the crisis. Subsumed under the bare statistics on the rise in poverty and unemployment is the fact that economic desperation will drive the poor towards actions that inflict harm on themselves and society at large. A case in point is the withdrawal of children from school in order to send them out to earn whatever they can, by whatever means. This not only compromises the future of the children involved but also undermines such important social objectives as the elimination of child labour and education for all. Of even greater concern is the moral harm of the forced marketization of inalienable rights through recourse to prostitution and hazardous work.

Most directly, the rise in poverty will mean damaging material deprivation. For the poor in a country like Indonesia this has already meant hunger and malnutrition. Longer-term costs arise from the permanent damage done by malnutrition in stunting the mental and physical development of children. The increased vulnerability to ill health arising from material deprivation will occur in a context where the private means to purchase and the public capacity to provide health services are declining sharply. The private capacity to purchase health services is greatly reduced by the twin pressures of falling incomes and the sharply increased costs of imported medicaments and medical supplies as a result of huge currency devaluations. At the same time, public provision of health services will also come under pressure due to rising costs, foreign exchange shortages, and declining government revenues as a result of the economic downturn.

Notes and references

[1] ILO/UNDP, 1998, p. 24.
[2] Warburg Dillon Read, 1998, p. 2.
[3] ILO/UNDP, 1998, p. 39.

CONTAINING THE SOCIAL COSTS

3

3.1 INITIAL SOURCES OF RELIEF

What could the millions of job losers and the new poor enumerated in the previous chapter expect by way of socially provided relief? The sad answer is, of course, "very little". A quick glance at table 3.1 is enough to confirm that, apart from the Republic of Korea, no other country in the table has unemployment insurance. Even in the Republic of Korea, the newness of the scheme (started in 1995) and its limited initial scope meant that in January 1998 unemployment benefit was paid to only 18,000 out of the then total of 900,000 unemployed persons. Coverage has since been extended substantially but the fact remains that very few of the first wave of job losers could count on this form of income support.

Those who were previously in regular employment could expect severance pay varying from two to six months of salary in the countries shown in table 3.1, although this was not always assured. Illiquid or bankrupt companies did not always meet their obligations, a fact attested to by the number of complaints over the non-payment of severance pay in the Labour Courts in Thailand since the crisis onset. This has been recognized as a serious problem in both Thailand and the Republic of Korea,[1] where special funds have recently been set up to guarantee the payment of severance pay. Even if all severance pay obligations were met in full it cannot escape notice that the sums involved will not stretch very far in a crisis that has lasted for over a year and is likely to drag on.

Retrenched workers could withdraw their balance of accumulated savings from state-run provident funds mainly designed to provide for retirement benefits. Again, this is an option only available to 12 and 16 per cent of the employed in Indonesia and Thailand respectively. In the Republic of Korea, less than 40 per cent of the employed contributed to the social security fund in 1997. However, even those who have this option cannot draw much comfort from it, since it involves jeopardizing old-age security for current survival. Many have been driven to take this step in desperation. It has been estimated that 15 per cent of the membership of the national provident fund in Indonesia will withdraw their balances in 1998, a fivefold increase over 1997.[2] In Thailand the corresponding estimated figure is 8.5 per cent.[3] It is also relevant to note that in Indonesia the average balance per worker in the national provident fund was very small (the equivalent of US$22) in 1997, hardly a source of great relief and more or less the result of poor management and inappropriate use of social security funds.[4]

Table 3.1. Aspects of social protection, 1997

	Unemployment insurance	Severance pay (months of salary)	Social security coverage Total employment (%)
Rep. of Korea	×	n.a.	38
Indonesia	○	4	12
Thailand	○	6	16
Malaysia	○	n.a.	48
Philippines	○	3	24
Hong Kong, China	○	2	n.a.
Singapore	○	0	80

× = yes. ○ = no. n.a. = not available.

Source: U.S. Government, *Social Security Programmes Throughout the World – 1997*, on Website: http://www.ssa.gov/statistics/ssptw97.html.

Most of the countries shown in table 3.1 have some rudimentary form of social assistance but, with the exception of Hong Kong, China, this is confined to those who are unable to work and not available to the unemployed. In any case the benefits, even in the case of the Republic of Korea, provide for little more than bare subsistence.

Apart from the above, at the onset of the crisis there was nothing else by way of socially provided relief to which victims of the crisis could turn. It should be borne in mind that the unemployed faced not only a loss of income but also of work-related benefits such as health insurance.

3.2 NEW SOCIAL EXPENDITURES

The harshness of the situation has been moderated somewhat since the early days of the crisis but socially provided relief is still far short of requirements. The suddenness of the onset of the crisis and the fact that its depth and duration were underestimated until a few months ago contributed to the slowness and limited size of the initial response. It will be recalled that the initial IMF programmes in Thailand, the Republic of Korea and Indonesia called for fiscal tightening that allowed little room for increased social expenditures. It was only the force of subsequent events – the deeper than anticipated recession, the swiftly mounting job losses, the accumulating indications of widespread social distress and unrest – that induced a change in policy. Fiscal targets were revised to allow room for increased social spending. This was most pronounced in Indonesia where a substantial fiscal deficit of 8.5 per cent of GDP was allowed for in the revised *Letter of Intent*, signed in June 1998,[5] in the immediate aftermath of the serious rioting and political agitation that led to the fall of President Suharto in May. In Thailand the target fiscal deficit was increased to 3 per cent of GDP in May[6] while in the Republic of Korea it was raised from 1.75 to 4 per cent of GDP in July.[7] These changes contrast sharply with the targets of a fiscal surplus of around 1 per cent of GDP when the IMF programmes were first agreed with Thailand, the Republic of Korea and Indonesia in the second half of 1997. This loosening of fiscal policy was not, of course, motivated solely by the need to increase social expenditures. Fiscal stimuli were needed to moderate the unforeseen depth of the contraction in the real economies of these countries, especially since monetary policy could not be eased within the macroeconomic framework agreed with the IMF.

Nonetheless, this loosening of fiscal policy has been accompanied by substantial increases in expenditures on mitigating the negative social effects of the crisis. Part of this increase reflects additional foreign assistance earmarked for social expenditures. This was most pronounced in Indonesia, where the entire deficit will be financed by additional foreign aid pledged in July 1998. Both the World Bank and the Asian Development Bank have also granted large social-sector loans to Thailand and Indonesia. Table 3.2 shows the latest position with respect to such expenditures, compiled from the most recent *Letters of Intent* available at the time of writing.

The first point to note is that not all of the increased expenditure made possible by the larger fiscal deficits has gone into social relief. In Thailand social expenditures amount to only half of the projected fiscal deficit of 3 per cent of GDP while in the Republic of Korea the corresponding proportion is 62.5 per cent. It is only in Indonesia that an amount equal to almost 90 per cent of the increased deficit spending will be devoted to social relief.

There are also significant differences between these countries in the social relief strategies they have adopted. In Indonesia, almost three-quarters of the total expenditures will be allocated to subsidizing the prices of essential goods and to ensuring that "sufficient quantities of essential foodstuffs are made available through the State Logistics Agency (BULOG) to the market".[8] The subsidies are intended "to stabilize the domestic prices of rice, soybeans, sugar, wheat flour, corn, soybean meal, and fishmeal, which account for a large part of the expenditure of poor households. In addition, the Government will temporarily freeze the prices of kerosene, gasoline, diesel, electricity and essential medicines."[9] This focus is explained by the fact that, unlike Thailand and the Republic of Korea, inflation is a serious problem in Indonesia. It has been the major factor behind the massive rise in poverty, provoking widespread social unrest and political instability; stabilizing the prices of essential commodities is clearly an attempt to defuse the tension. This focus, of course, leaves little room for other measures, of which there are two: only a relatively modest public works programme and grants for school fees. In contrast to the Indonesian situation, the programmes in Thailand and the Republic of Korea are more diversified.

In both Thailand and the Republic of Korea a significant part of total social expenditure is allocated for employment creation, reflecting the fact that unemployment is the major source of their social problems. Apart from employment creation, other measures directed at relieving the plight of the unemployed are the considerable extension of coverage for unemployment insurance and the provision of loans to the unemployed in the Republic of Korea; and the continuation of social security coverage for previous contributors who have lost their jobs in Thailand. Other social concerns, such as the crisis-induced drop-outs from the educational system and the reduced access to health care, are also addressed in Thailand.

What proportion of those in need have been, or will be, helped by these measures? It is difficult to give a clear-cut, overall answer owing to the varied mix of assistance on offer. Each caters to a different aspect of deprivation, (health care, employment, schooling) and each reaches different numbers. Some forms of assistance also clearly overlap, since more than one form can be received at the same time by the same beneficiary. An approximative answer can be supplied for perhaps the key instrument of assistance, employment creation. Table 3.2 lists the expenditures on direct employment creation and estimates the number of jobs that will be offered. The estimates can be compared with the number of unemployed to gauge the adequacy of what is on offer. This comparison gives the depressing result that only a small proportion of the unemployed can expect relief through public employment-creation schemes. In Thailand only 7 per cent and in Indonesia (at best) 10 per cent of the unemployed can expect to obtain a job in these schemes. This figure is much higher in the Republic of Korea, where approximately 24 per cent of the unemployed are able to count on this form of employment. The fact that a growing proportion of the unemployed in the Republic of Korea will now, or soon will, be receiving unemployment benefits makes the contrast with the situation in Thailand and Indonesia even more striking.

Table 3.2. Crisis-induced social expenditures, 1998/99

	Total expenditure (Billion $)	(% GDP)	Expenditure on employment creation (billion $)		Estimated no. of jobs created (man years)	Other measures
Thailand	2.3	1.5	Supplementary support for existing job-creation programmes	0.1	17 000	Increased severance pay from 6 months to maximum of 10 months for those with >10 years service
			Rural industrial employment	0.003	3 000	Extending social security coverage from 6 to 12 months for unemployed workers who were contributing to social security fund when employed (100,000 workers)
			Urban Development Fund	0.06	11 000	Extending health care coverage (4.5 million persons)
			Infrastructure projects in urban and rural areas by state enterprises	1.25	100 000*	Training (120,000 workers)
						Student loans and scholarships (300,000 beneficiaries)
Indonesia	15.7	7.5% of which subsidizes food, fuel electricity and medicine equal to 6% of GDP		1.0	1 000 000	School fees grants
Rep. of Korea	7.6	2.5	Job creation	2.4	380 000	Extending coverage of unemployment insurance from firms with >5 workers to all firms and to part-time and temporary workers
						Loans to unemployed
						Social assistance

* Author's estimate based on cost per job is double that for the other schemes, as this item seems to be large-scale infrastructure projects.

Sources: 1. Thailand. *Letter of Intent*, May 26 1998 and August 25 1998. 2. Indonesia: *Letter of Intent*, June 24, 1998. 3. Rep. of Korea: *Letter of Intent*, July 24, 1998.

A fundamental issue that arises from looking at these programmes is whether they can properly be called "social safety nets", the term that has been used by the Bretton Woods institutions and the governments concerned. Strictly speaking, since these programmes do not provide basic income support to all who seek it (and are verified as claimants in genuine need by some form of means test), the term is inaccurate when applied to these countries. In industrialized countries the role played by social assistance constitutes a genuine social safety net. In contrast, programmes discussed here provide relief to only a fraction of those in need, as was shown in the case of public employment. In addition, they cover only some contingencies, such as a disrupted access to health care or education, and do not provide basic income support.

This point is raised because it involves more than just a semantic quibble. It does, in fact, impinge on the basic issue of whether the strategies that have been adopted have been optimal. An important aspect of this is the question of how the particular priorities for assistance were arrived at. There are a host of competing needs to be met at a time of mass social distress and difficult choices must be made. However, in the absence of information on the criteria for choice that were used, one cannot help but wonder if some alternative strategy might not have made better sense. In the case of Thailand and Indonesia, the principal alternative could have been to concentrate resources on providing employment in a public scheme to all who sought it. This would have assured universality of access to those in need. If the wage offered is set at subsistence level the scheme would have been self-targeting, since only those in extreme need would offer themselves for such work. This would circumvent the central problem inherent in providing public assistance, which is screening out the non-genuine claimants. Another alternative would have been to put heavier reliance on passive measures such as expanded social assistance. Admittedly, this would have been difficult to put in place quickly, given that the administrative capacity to verify claims did not exist. But it does have the advantage of being less costly than active measures such as public employment schemes which entail expenditures on equipment, materials and project administration.

If we abstract from the problem of feasibility then there should be little doubt that a heavier reliance on passive income support would have been desirable. This follows from the sharp contrast between what the Republic of Korea has been able to achieve and the situation in Indonesia and Thailand. As has been commented upon earlier, a substantially higher proportion of those in need in the Republic of Korea have been covered by the combination of active and passive measures. This has been achieved with expenditures amounting to no more that 2.5 per cent of GDP, which is substantially lower than the level in Indonesia and not greatly above that in Thailand. A major factor that made this possible was that the Republic of Korea had introduced unemployment insurance two years before the crisis and, therefore, the scope of the initially limited system could be successively extended during the course of the crisis. It could thus rely on the easier option of providing passive income support when the other two countries could not. This leads us to the counterfactual point that if Thailand and Indonesia had also introduced unemployment insurance prior to the crisis they could have coped better with the social consequences of the crisis. By its very nature this is a point that is difficult to prove, but independently of this, there are arguments in favour of the introduction of unemployment insurance in these countries which will be presented in Chapter 4.

3.3 THE WEAKNESS OF SOCIAL INSTITUTIONS

The weakness of the existing systems of social protection when the crisis hit, as well as the limitations of social programmes introduced by the governments thereafter, are linked, in part, to the fact that labour institutions were also poorly developed in several of the crisis-affected countries. As will be seen in table 3.3, trade union density is extremely low in Indonesia and Thailand and only somewhat higher in the Republic of Korea and Malaysia. Even more significant is the fact that the ratification rate of the ILO core Convention on Freedom of Association (No. 87) is extremely low. Of the seven countries shown in table 3.3 only the Philippines and Hong Kong, China, have ratified this Convention. Interestingly enough, these are also the countries with the highest trade union densities within the group. While non-ratification is not always an indication of hostility to trade union rights, the record of some of the non-ratifying countries under the ILO supervisory machinery for this Convention suggests that there have been problems.[10] Moreover, some of the public rhetoric on "Asian values" by the leaders of some of these countries reveals strong reservations over the universality of fundamental democratic rights, of which freedom of association is an important part. All this suggests that, to say the least, there has not been any enthusiasm for the development of a free and independent trade union movement in some of these countries. As a consequence, institutions for industrial relations from the enterprise level upwards remain poorly developed.

As pointed out in a recent ILO review of industrial relations in Asia, "for a long time authoritarian power took the place of industrial relations. With industrial development, a rise in education standards and the dawn of democracy, the need for sounder collective bargaining made itself felt in some countries. This was the case in the Republic of Korea ... The fact remains, however, that the mechanisms which facilitate social dialogue are, on the whole, still underdeveloped ... The proportion of employees covered by collective agreement rarely exceeds 4 per cent in

Table 3.3. Trade union density and ratification of ILO Conventions on Freedom of Association (No. 87) and the Right to Organize and Collective Bargaining (No. 98)

	Trade union membership as % of non-agricultural labour force (1995)	Ratification of Freedom of Association and Right to Organize and Collective Bargaining (as of Feb. 98)	
		Convention 87	Convention 98
Rep. of Korea	9.0	–	–
Indonesia	2.6	–	×
Thailand	3.1	–	–
Malaysia	11.7	–	×
Philippines	22.8	×	×
Hong Kong, China	18.5	×	×
Singapore	13.5	–	×

× = yes.

Source: ILO: *World Labour Report 1997-98*, Statistical Annex: Table 1.2 and Table 5.

most countries of the region."[11] Similarly, institutions for tripartite consultations on labour, social and economic issues remain poorly developed. "In Malaysia, Thailand and Sri Lanka, the role of tripartism is limited, either because the tripartite commissions seldom meet or because their conclusions have little effect."[12] Moreover, "in some cases the unions' powerlessness to act at the national level is the result of a legal prohibition. In Malaysia, the national unions are incorporated only as 'societies' to facilitate relations among workers, and have no bargaining powers, which are granted exclusively to enterprise unions."[13]

These institutional lacunae have proved a liability during the current crisis. An important loss was the inability to find cooperative labour-management mechanisms for confronting the economic problems posed by the severity of the crisis. As mentioned in Chapter 1, many fundamentally sound enterprises faced crisis-induced problems of illiquidity and some of them could have bought valuable breathing space to ride it out, by negotiating with unions for the adoption of alternatives to liquidation and lay-offs (such as the recourse to reduced working time, work-sharing, and negotiated wage cuts). Viable enterprises would have been rescued and the moderation of lay-offs would have benefited employers, workers and governments alike. The weakness of industrial-relations institutions in Thailand and Indonesia prevented this from happening to any significant extent.[14] It was only in the Republic of Korea, where unions are stronger and industrial relations institutions more developed, that this option was more fully utilized.

The second cardinal opportunity missed as a result of institutional underdevelopment was that of using tripartite mechanisms, involving government and workers' and employers' organizations, to secure social consensus on economic reform programmes and measures for containing the social costs of the crisis. The primary value of social consensus lies in the fact that it is a powerful means for averting the social unrest which often arises in times of economic crisis. Such unrest typically leads to an aggravation of the crisis and retards economic reform and recovery. Tripartite agreements can avert this because they represent a fair compromise between competing demands which all interest groups involved in the negotiations can therefore support. From the standpoint of labour, the value of tripartite agreements is that they typically deliver better social protection from the ravages of a crisis than would otherwise have been the case. As discussed earlier, the inadequacy of the policy response to the social problems created by the present crisis has indeed been a grave cause for concern.

Here again the contrast between the Republic of Korea and the other two countries (Thailand and Indonesia) is instructive. In the Republic of Korea a Tripartite Social accord was signed in February 1998, a few months after the onset of the crisis. This accord constituted the basis for the strong response to the social costs of the crisis as previously mentioned.[15] These included the extension of the unemployment insurance system and the introduction of an impressive array of active labour market measures. Nothing of similar importance occurred in Thailand and Indonesia, principally owing to their substantially weaker labour movements.

3.4 CONCLUDING REMARKS

The preceding discussion has shown that while there has been clear concern over the social impact of the economic crisis and even though this has been manifested in a range of initiatives to contain social costs, the overall impression must be that the response so far has been inadequate. In particular, efforts to cater for the large numbers of displaced workers cover only a small fraction of those in need of such relief. In addition, except in the Republic of Korea, there has been virtually no temporary income support, either in the form of unemployment benefits or social assistance, to compensate for the shortfall in the coverage of direct employment-creation measures.

There are two fundamental reasons why the worst-affected countries are in their current state of social distress. The first is the sheer magnitude of the social fallout from an unexpected and severe economic crisis. This would, in and of itself, have put serious stress even on countries with better-developed systems of social protection. The second reason is the underdevelopment of systems of social protection and of institutions for collective bargaining and social dialogue.

This suggests that a two-pronged approach is required to overcome the current social distress. The first is to try to bring about an economic recovery as soon as possible so that the numbers in need of relief can be reduced through a steady reabsorption into income-earning activities. This necessitates priority attention to economic policies and related structural reforms for promoting recovery. At the same time, however, work on the second prong of strengthening systems of social protection and labour institutions must also begin. Since high and sustained growth can clearly no longer be taken for granted, a significantly greater degree of social protection must be aimed for. Just as the Great Depression forged a new social contract in many industrialized countries in the 1930s, so too must the current Asian crisis serve as an impetus to creating a more socially oriented model of development. Chapter 4 seeks to point the way forward.

Notes and references

[1] ILO, 1998a, pp. 43-44.

[2] ibid., p. 43.

[3] ILO, 1998b.

[4] ILO, 1998a, p. 26.

[5] Indonesia: *Letter of Intent*, 24 June 1998, available from IMF Website: http://www.imf.org/external/np/loi/062498.htm.

[6] Thailand: *Letter of Intent*, 26 May 1998, available from IMF Website: http://www.imf.org/external/np/loi/052698.htm.

[7] The Republic of Korea: *Letter of Intent*, 24 July 1998, available from IMF Website: http://www.imf.org/external/np/loi/072498.htm.

[8] Indonesia: *Letter of Intent*, 24 June 1998, Annex I, available from IMF Website: http://www.imf.org/external/np/loi/062498.htm.

[9] ibid.

[10] ILO, 1998a, pp. 52-55.

[11] ILO, 1997b, pp. 164-165.

[12] ibid.

[13] ibid., p. 168.

[14] ibid., pp. 33-35.

[15] See ibid, pp. 45-46, for fuller details.

THE CHALLENGE FOR SOCIAL POLICY

4

This chapter looks beyond the current preoccupation with social costs and policies to contain them and concentrates on some broad lessons for future policy. The focus is on the need to strengthen policies and institutions over the medium term in order to reduce the risk of similar crises in the future and to improve the level of social protection.

4.1 ECONOMIC AND POLITICAL REFORM

An obvious priority is to press ahead with the structural reforms that have been initiated in the wake of the crisis. Of key importance is the strengthening of the financial system which proved itself to be the Achilles heel of the pre-crisis economic system. In a world of increasingly integrated financial markets, a sound and resilient financial system is an essential buffer against the continuing danger of economic crisis. It is also indispensable for ensuring a return to high and stable growth in the post-crisis period. Similar observations apply to weaknesses in corporate governance that have been exposed by the crisis.

In large part, achieving reform will involve technical measures to correct deficiencies such as poor and opaque accounting, lax prudential supervision of banks and the absence of effective bankruptcy laws. But wider new issues relating to the regulation of markets in the context of increasing integration into the global economy will also have to be faced. These relate in particular to the need to find effective instruments to control the degree of exposure to foreign debt by private economic agents, to set prudent limits to debt/equity ratios in the corporate sector and to discourage speculative and unproductive investment.

These technical measures of institutional strengthening and regulation are absolutely essential but by no means sufficient. It was not only weaknesses in formal institutions that created the preconditions for the crisis, but also the contamination of market processes by politics. Unless the latter is contained, no amount of tinkering with institutions and regulatory mechanisms will be to much avail.

The strengthening of democratic institutions is central to the post-crisis economic model that is required. Free and fair electoral processes, freedom of expression and public debate, the rule of law, and account-ability of elected officials are among the attributes of democracy that are essential for preventing the harmful distortion of market processes by arbitrary government intervention and corruption. The recent crisis has shown such arbitrariness to have not only high economic but also social costs. Thus, the intrinsic value of democracy is strongly reinforced by socio-economic considerations.

Democracy is also essential for ensuring greater social equity in the development process. As has been commented upon earlier, there had been a relative neglect of labour rights and social protection in the pre-crisis period of high growth. The negative consequences of this neglect have been dramatically revealed by the extreme social pain that has been suffered since the onset of the crisis. An essential element for correcting this deficiency is the widest possible involvement of those concerned, through their representative organizations, in the definition and imple-mentation of measures to overcome the crisis and minimize its social effects. This will ensure constant democratic pressure to improve working conditions and levels of social protection. It will be invaluable in achieving a smooth adjustment to structural change, in coping with economic and social crises and in raising productivity and competitive-ness. A crucial requirement will be the fostering of a strong and free labour movement and the building up of a solid system of industrial relations. Most of the crisis-affected countries have a relatively poor record on this score; their political leaders continue to doubt the value of freedom of association and the positive role that trade unions can play in fostering equitable development. It is therefore important to confront these doubts in the following section. This will present a rights-based argument in favour of freedom of association (that is unavoidably abstract and philosophical), followed by a necessary corrective to misplaced (but, regrettably, over-influential) fears about the negative economic impact of trade union rights. Although these arguments are cast generically, they are nevertheless highly germane to the present conjuncture in the crisis-affected countries of East and South-East Asia.

4.2 THE IMPORTANCE OF FREEDOM OF ASSOCIATION

Freedom of association and the right to organize are recognized as part of basic human rights. The right of workers and employers "to establish and ... to join organizations of their own choosing without previous authorization"[1] is an important democratic right. It is on the same level as the right to associate freely in the political sphere and is closely linked to basic political rights such as freedom of expression, of assembly, and from arbitrary arrest. In fact, the exercise of freedom of association would not be possible in a context where basic political rights are violated. Not surprisingly, therefore, "the status of workers' rights in a country is a bellwether for the status of human rights in general ... Repressive regimes inevitably attempt to suppress or control trade unions; thus labour leaders are among the most frequent victims of repression. Conversely, the development of free trade unions signals the dissolution of authoritarian regimes."[2] Freedom of association and the right to organize are key components of international action to promote democracy and full respect of basic human rights.

Yet their acceptance is far from wholehearted and universal. The diffidence comes not only from those who contest the universality and primacy of basic political and civil rights but also from those who embrace neo-liberal economic doctrines. The former see these rights as impediments to economic development while the latter are concerned about the negative impact of trade unions on economic efficiency and equity. These are both consequentialist arguments, based on claims about the effects of rights on economic outcomes. While "advocates of moral rights often see them as unconditional and uncompromising – independently of consequences,"[3] it would be unwise to ignore such consequentialist arguments entirely. This is because the "the political and social acceptability of a moral right – and of course its effectiveness – must depend to a considerable extent on its ability to be persuasive. Cutting the consequential link can reduce – rather than enhance its status – as well as its following, and also compromise its reach."[4] In this spirit, it will be argued that neither source of doubt over basic rights as described above is really justified.

Asian values and the universality of human rights

Questioning the universality of basic civil and political rights, which include freedom of association and the right to organize, has come mainly from some East Asian countries. This consists of a "cultural relativist" claim that there are distinct "Asian values" (which place communitarian values and social harmony above individual rights) that are just as legitimate as Western-inspired concepts of human rights. The claim has not, however, stood up to critical scrutiny. The main counterarguments are that there is no evidence that Asian thought and tradition have historically given less importance to civil and political freedoms; that it is difficult to identify values intrinsically common to the large and diverse continent of Asia; and that the case has been articulated by authoritarian regimes and does not therefore represent an expression of popular will.[5]

This essentially value-based argument has been augmented by a related *instrumental* argument to the effect that basic civil and political rights are harmful for development. The claim is that successful development requires a strong authoritarian state which would be undermined by a premature commitment to individual liberties. This is buttressed by a parallel claim that socio-economic rights such as the right to subsistence and to development are far more important than individual liberties which are luxuries that poor countries can ill afford.

These claims do not stand up to scrutiny either. "Systematic statistical studies give no real support to the claim that there is a general conflict between political rights and economic performance. That relationship seems to depend on many other circumstances, and while some note a weakly negative relation, others find a strongly positive one. On balance, the hypothesis that there is not much relation between them in either direction is hard to reject. Since these rights have importance of their own, the case for them stands, even without having to show that democracy actually encourages economic growth."[6]

The parallel claim that socio-economic rights should take precedence over civil and political rights is based on the notion that "any meaningful exercise of civil and political rights depends on the attainment of social-economic rights, and so must be deferred until the latter have been realized. In the words of one Chinese government statement, "The right to subsistence is the most important of all human rights, without which the other rights are out of the question."[7]

While not denying the obvious truth that basic material well-being is a precondition for the exercise of basic civil and political rights, it is invalid to project this as an argument for deferring these rights until socio-economic rights are attained. First, as pointed out earlier, there is no evidence of a conflict between civil and political rights, on the one hand, and the possibilities for economic and social progress, on the other. There is thus no case for deferring civil and political rights on these grounds. Second, "at least a subset of civil and political rights is indispensable for securing basic subsistence rights (if not all socio-economic rights) and therefore essential to life and dignity."[8] A case in point is the "connection between political and civil rights, on the one hand, and the prevention of major social disasters and misfortunes on the other."[9] This is because "it is very hard for any government to go to the polls after a major social calamity, nor can it easily survive criticism from the media and opposition parties, in a functioning democracy."[10] Basic civil and political rights, and among them trade union rights, are an important safeguard against the social and economic injustice that represses the living standards of the poor.

It is also relevant to note that there is no basis for arguing that poor countries cannot afford to implement basic civil and political rights.

These are for the most part "negative rights", in the sense that what is required is for governments to refrain from obstructing the free exercise of these rights. This is clearly the case with respect to freedom of association and the right to organize.

There is thus no convincing argument, on the grounds of either cultural relativism or developmental imperatives, to deny basic civil and political rights, including fundamental trade union rights. But this does not clinch the issue: the implicit reticence towards trade union rights (deriving from neo-liberal economic arguments) also needs to be examined.

Trade unions and economic performance

The general neo-liberal view of trade unions is that they are the root cause of labour market distortions from which many negative economic consequences flow. These include the raising of labour costs above market clearing levels, thereby reducing competitiveness and employment; the creation of obstacles to flexible adjustment within enterprises; the undermining of macroeconomic stability through excessive wage settlements; and the disruption of industrial peace. In addition to these arguments on the grounds of economic efficiency is the oft-repeated argument on the grounds of equity. It is contended that trade unions increase income-inequality between members and non-members, both directly through the union wage-premium and indirectly through negative effects on the employment prospects of non-members. This argument is wielded with particular force in the developing countries, where unionized labour is depicted as a small "labour aristocracy" that depresses the income and employment prospects of the vast majority of workers.

The case against unions on the grounds that they distort efficiency is, however, rarely pushed to the point of denying freedom of association. The reason is that this issue first surfaced in advanced industrial democracies where even the most ardent free marketeers cannot find a convincing moral basis for denying the fundamental human right of freedom of association. Instead, they seek to reduce trade union influence, to privilege individual rights over collective rights in labour relations, and to achieve greater "flexibility" by reducing the extent of regulation of the labour market and the level of welfare benefits.

The continuing debate over this issue defines a major divide in policy attitudes towards trade union rights. On one side is the neo-liberal view that, while trade unions have a right to exist, the legal and institutional framework should not confer on them a privileged role in wage bargaining and corporate governance and should certainly not grant them any of the political power and attributes of the State through, for example, national tripartite institutions. On the other side is the social democratic view that freedom of association would be an empty right if it were not accompanied by institutional arrangements that provide for trade union participation in governing the world of work and in influencing economic and social policies affecting the interests of workers. This position is based not only on a point of rights but on a belief that, contrary to the neo-liberal stance, such arrangements would lead to superior economic and social outcomes. These opposing concepts are the source of underlying tension in the interpretation of the scope and practical implications of the right to freedom of association, impinging on issues such as the right to strike and the appropriate balance between collective and individual rights.

It is therefore useful to examine the relative validity of these competing theories on what types of labour institution should develop from the base of freedom of association and the right to bargain collectively. The first issue that needs to be addressed is the robustness of the empirical evidence on the negative economic effects of trade unions.

As in the case of the earlier discussion on the relationship between human rights and development, there is no clear-cut empirical evidence to support the neo-liberal view of the economically harmful effects of trade unions. The main contention in the neo-liberal view, that greater labour market flexibility (associated with limited trade union influence and, by implication, lower union-inspired labour market regulation) is associated with superior economic performance, remains unproven.

Countries with very different labour market institutions have displayed similar degrees of success in terms of GDP growth and trade performance. Even with respect to employment performance, a key argument in the neo-liberal case, the evidence is far from convincing. The prime exhibit is the superior employment performance of the United States (representing flexible labour markets) compared with Europe (depicted as the epitome of labour market rigidity) since 1973. While this view has gained currency in policy circles and much of the financial press, its empirical basis is meagre. Contrary to popular stereotype, there has in fact been considerable intra-European variation in terms of employment performance. Moreover, this intra-European variation in employment performance is not correlated to differences in labour market institutions as predicted by neo-liberal theory. Other empirical tests of the relationship between specific features of labour market regulation and employment growth have also contradicted the predictions of the neo-liberal model.[11]

All this suggests that it is unconvincing to attribute a central role to labour market institutions in explaining differences in employment performance. Other factors, such as macroeconomic policy, the degree of regulation of product markets and the effectiveness of skill development and active labour market policies, are probably of greater significance. It is also important to note that a simple dichotomy between "rigid" and "flexible" labour markets overlooks a crucial dimension of the relationship between labour market institutions and economic performance. The fact is that the institutional arrangements determining the relationship between trade unions and employers' organizations and government, as well as the objectives and behaviour of trade unions and employers' organizations, are more decisive influences on economic outcomes than simpler indicators such as the extent of unionization or of labour market regulation.

Trade unions and equity

The view that trade unions increase inequality is even more difficult to sustain. Indeed, the primary rationale for trade unionism is precisely the reverse, that is, they decrease inequality through obtaining a fairer share of total product for labour through the exercise of countervailing market power. This is particularly true in situations where monopsony (a single buyer) is present in labour markets.

It is nonetheless possible that where unionized workers are a small minority and where unions opt for restrictive practices in the own narrow interests, there can be adverse indirect effects on equity and the employment prospects of non-unionized workers. However, in practice, this is often mitigated by the creation of tripartite institutions that provide incentives for unions to take into account overall economic and social interests; by trade union concern for, and their advocacy of, the interests of low-income and disadvantaged groups; and the trade union achievement of such social gains as national systems of social and labour protection which, in principle, benefit all workers. The policy requirement is to promote such pro-equity developments in the institutional environment rather than take the fatalistic view that trade unionism is automatically harmful to equity.

For the developing countries, these policy requirements remain basically the same. At low levels of per capita income, the size of the modern sector and hence of wage-employment is typically small. The potential extent of unionization will be low to begin with but this is not a convincing argument for discouraging the growth of trade unions. First, it is not necessarily true that unions in the modern sector will invariably work to establish a labour aristocracy. Even if there is an inherent tendency for them to do so, it can be tempered by policies such as the creation of tripartite institutions for social dialogue, wherein workers and employers can be persuaded to take into account broader economic and social interests. There is a moral case for balancing trade union rights with responsibilities. "Unionists ... owe moral duties to the remainder of the labouring classes, and moral duties to the community at large; and it behoves them to take care that the conditions they make for their own separate interest do not conflict with either of these obligations."[12] Second, since the key dynamic of development is the progressive expansion of the modern sector, the smallness of the potential labour force that can be unionized is a problem that will diminish over time. Third, given that freedom of association is a basic human right, there is no case for delaying its realization. A start has to be made at even the lowest levels of development. Over a century ago, John Stuart Mill said "The thing is scarcely to be done, if done at all, in any other way. National unionism must be built up piecemeal."[13]

The wider benefits of freedom of association

The narrow economic calculus that fears the negative effects of trade unions on development and on efficiency and equity disregards the wider benefits that flow from freedom of association. The first benefit is improvements in conditions of work, especially the elimination of inhumane practices, brought about by trade union activity. This is a vast welfare gain not only in terms of restoring human dignity to the erstwhile victims of these practices but also in eliminating morally unacceptable gulfs in the life-chances of individuals within the same society.

The second benefit is the contribution of freedom of association to the building of more democratic, participatory and equitable patterns of development which not only have intrinsic value in expanding "human freedom and capability"[14] but are also being increasingly recognized as the best route to successful development. Far from being simply a technical problem of economic policy, "Development represents a *transformation* of society, a movement away from traditional relations, traditional ways of thinking ... to more modern ways. ...Thus, if reforms intended to promote development are to transform entire societies, they must involve entire societies. This has led to an increasing concern over ownership and participation in development strategies, and in creating institutions which give expression to ownership and participation."[15] Participation in decision-making is, of course, essential for building consensus around policies and for ensuring their successful implementation. Freedom of association is a basic requirement for the development of such democratic and participatory institutions.

The third benefit of freedom of association is that it is an essential precondition for ensuring that economic and social policies will be responsive to popular demands for social justice. Without constant democratic pressure from workers' organizations to influence them, it is highly likely that these policies will be inequitable and fail to provide adequate levels of labour and social protection.

4.3 EMPLOYMENT POLICIES

Having dealt with the fundamental issue of labour institutions and democracy, we can now move on to discuss two key issues of economic and social policy. One priority is employment promotion, the other is the strengthening of social protection.

The crisis has raised the issue of whether it has also marked the end of an "easy phase" of employment creation based on exceptionally high rates of economic growth. If rates of economic growth in the post-crisis period do not return to previous trend levels, there will be a need to pay greater attention to policies for employment creation. Quite apart from this consideration, however, the crisis has also provided other strong reasons for a strengthening of employment policies.

A first reason is that the crisis has brought home the fact that a high rate of job creation is not sufficient in itself; policy-makers should also be concerned about the sustainability of the jobs that are created. When a significant misallocation of investment occurs, as was the case in the pre-crisis period, then the jobs linked to this misallocated investment are clearly at risk. Indeed, much of the job loss since the crisis onset has been in activities associated with an over-expanded construction and financial sector. The concern over the sustainability of job creation highlights the necessarily close links between economic and employment policy. A misallocation of investment is unwise in itself, for standard economic reasons. But it also sows seeds of fragility into the job creation system and this in turn has high potential social costs when, sooner or later, jobs are lost.

A second reason is that the crisis has revealed significant gaps in the institutional capacity to deal with issues of enterprise restructuring and mass lay-offs. Comprehensive information systems to provide advance warning of, and to monitor, mass lay-offs do not exist and this has proved a severe handicap to the formulation and implementation of countervailing measures. Moreover, there has clearly been a very limited capacity to implement active measures to facilitate the redeployment of laid-off workers, such as job-search assistance, retraining and mobility assistance. While it is true that such measures will apply mainly to redeployment within the modern sector, this does not mean that they should be neglected. Even in the countries that still have high levels of rural and informal sector employment (Thailand and Indonesia), such measures can play a significant role as part of the overall response to a sudden onset of mass lay-offs. In the post-crisis period, the weight of modern-sector employment will undoubtedly continue to grow and with it the need for a stronger institutional capacity to design and implement active labour market policies.

A third reason is that the crisis has also revealed limitations in the institutional capacity to scale-up existing programmes, such as public works and the promotion of self-employment in the rural and informal sectors, to meet the greatly increased need for such assistance during periods of economic crisis.

A major effort of institutional development is therefore required to remedy these deficiencies. In this respect, two areas deserve special emphasis. First is the need to create stronger capacities to monitor and evaluate the employment implications of overall economic policies. This will involve strengthening the research and policy analysis functions of labour ministries and the establishment of close working links between labour and economic ministries. The remit of this employment policy cluster within government should be to ensure that economic policies do not contain distortions that hinder employment creation or divert it into non-sustainable directions. In general, job creation should be in line with the underlying comparative advantage of the economy and markets should be open and competitive, subject to the need to correct market failures. Of particular importance is a policy, legal and regulatory environment that facilitates the creation and development of competitive enterprises.

The second area that deserves special emphasis is the strengthening of public employment services, in particular their capacity to design and implement active labour market policies. Parallel capacity-building will be required in those agencies responsible for designing and implementing direct employment creation schemes. In this context, employment-intensive investment programmes targeted at the unemployed and the underemployed are major considerations. Similarly, agencies responsible for the promotion of self-employment in the rural and informal sectors and the development of entrepreneurship and promoting micro-, small- and medium-sized enterprises also need to be strengthened.

4.4 THE CASE FOR INTRODUCING UNEMPLOYMENT INSURANCE

The absence of unemployment benefits in the crisis-affected countries has inflicted unnecessary suffering and hardship. Although an unemployment insurance scheme would not have relieved all the social pain induced by the crisis, its contribution would nevertheless have been substantial. As shown in Chapter 2, most of the job loss was concentrated in the modern sector and it is precisely this group of workers that unemployment insurance would have covered. Had coverage been extensive enough, say extending to all employees in enterprises with more than five workers, then a majority of job losers would have been eligible for unemployment benefits. This would have alleviated the shock and distress suffered by these workers and would have attenuated social tensions and unrest. In addition, the payment of these benefits would have made some contribution, albeit a very small one, to containing the fall in domestic demand. In other words, the unemployment insurance system would have also functioned as an automatic stabilizer.

Some false beliefs

In the face of these obvious benefits it is a puzzle why, apart from the Republic of Korea, none of these countries had introduced any form of unemployment insurance. It is all the more puzzling in the case of Singapore and Hong Kong, China, where per capita GDP is higher than in many OECD countries. There is no direct information on which to base a firm answer to the question of why unemployment insurance was not introduced. The first of several reasons is that, given decades of uninterrupted full employment, the risk of unemployment was perceived as slight, both by governments and workers. In the tight labour markets that prevailed, unemployment was a rare occurrence. When it did occur, spells of unemployment were brief and the need for an unemployment insurance system was thus small. A second and related reason, applying mainly to countries with large agricultural and informal sectors such as Indonesia and Thailand, is that there was excessive faith in the capacity of these sectors to absorb retrenched workers. This faith in the role of traditional safety net mechanisms probably contributed to a downplaying of the problems posed by open unemployment. A third reason was the belief that a system of unemployment benefits would not be feasible in developing countries. This was based on perceptions that the fiscal costs were too high, that the administrative capacity to operate such schemes was lacking, and that the predominance of small enterprises in the industrial structure made these schemes inherently difficult to implement. A fourth reason was ideological hostility to the concept of the welfare state. As discussed earlier, champions of "Asian values" decry what they see as the erosion of the work ethic and the social pathologies caused by generous welfare provision in advanced Western countries. According to this view, unemployment benefits feature as a major part of the problem and are consequently to be avoided. Related to this are the standard apprehensions of free marketeers about the negative effects of unemployment benefits on employment. These include the raising of labour costs, and hence the reduction of the willingness of employers to hire, if the system is financed through payroll taxes; the weakening of the incentive to seek work; the raising of the reservation wage (the wage necessary to induce a worker to accept a job);[16] and the reduction in the demand for labour through higher wage costs brought about by the fact that the presence of unemployment benefits makes it less costly for workers to quit their jobs more frequently and that, as a consequence, employers have to pay higher wages to counteract this.[17] A final reason probably relates to the weakness of trade unions and the restraints on freedom of association in several of these countries. In the industrialized countries, trade unions had been the most powerful pressure group demanding the introduction of unemployment benefits. The weakness of the trade union movement in some South-East Asian countries meant the absence of similar pressure.

Most of the above putative explanations for the failure to introduce a system of unemployment benefits also constitute arguments against the introduction of unemployment insurance that need to be confronted. The easiest argument to refute is that the risk of unemployment is low and that there is little need for unemployment insurance. The dramatic rise in unemployment in the wake of the crisis documented in Chapter 2 has shattered this cosy assumption. Moreover, there is no room for retreat to the argument that the crisis was a one-off event that will not recur. Economic reforms and better economic management may reduce the future risk of a recurrence but cannot eliminate it entirely, especially in a context where economic volatility and the frequency of financial crises have been increasing in the global economy. There are also grounds for assuming that unemployment will loom as a larger problem over the next few years than in the past in South-East Asian countries. First, there is the fact that the restructuring of enterprises is a process that will need to continue until these countries eliminate excess capacity in some industries and seek to regain competitiveness. Second, when economic recovery is achieved there will be a continual need to adjust the structure of production to ever-changing comparative advantage, especially through upgrading to more skill- and capital-intensive production as per capita income and labour costs rise. Both these processes will imply the relocation of labour and some rise in unemployment unless the extraordinarily high growth rates of the pre-crisis period are regained. It should be noted here that one of the side-benefits of an unemployment benefit system is that it facilitates the process of industrial restructuring, since the added economic security it provides reduces the resistance of workers to change.

The sharp rise in open unemployment in the wake of the crisis, even in countries with such large agricultural and informal sectors as Thailand and Indonesia, should sweep away any lingering illusions about the adequacy of traditional safety nets. Moreover, the trend towards a weakening of the capacity of the rural and informal sectors to absorb retrenched workers will continue as commercialization and productivity growth in agriculture proceeds and as the urban informal sector shrinks with rising per capita income. The need for a system of unemployment benefits will increase with this decline in the relative size and labour-absorptive capacity of the agricultural and informal sectors.

Turning to more substantive issues, we shall first address the question of the affordability and the feasibility of unemployment insurance before considering possible costs in terms of negative effects on the functioning of the labour market.

The issue of affordability

An unemployment insurance scheme is, as the name implies, typically self-financing. It is based on the compulsory pooling of risk and is financed by contributions of either workers or employers or a combination of both. The question of affordability in the sense of a fiscal cost need not therefore arise unless the government chooses to subsidize the scheme. This is a fundamental difference between the insurance scheme being advocated here and state-funded systems based on general revenues.

The basic rationale for an insurance scheme is that it is a means for overcoming several market failures. One is the tendency for workers to underestimate the risk of becoming unemployed and hence to under-provide for this eventuality through savings.[18] Another is the absence of a private market for unemployment insurance due to the problem of asymmetric information.[19] The probability of becoming unemployed differs among individuals but this is difficult for insurance companies to gauge. It is therefore impossible to run a scheme that relates the level of the premium individuals are charged to their specific risk of becoming unemployed. The only practicable scheme is a common premium for all, based on the average probability of becoming unemployed. Such a scheme would, however, run into the problem of adverse selection; only those facing a higher than average risk of becoming unemployed would be willing to subscribe to the scheme, thus undermining its financial viability.[20] Without state intervention there would be inadequate provision against the contingency of unemployment; individuals do not provide enough cover on their own and, because private provision is not viable, they cannot surmount this by buying insurance. A state-run unemployment insurance scheme overcomes these market failures by making participation mandatory, thereby overcoming both the problem of individual underprovision and of adverse selection.

Given that the scheme can be self-financing, the only real issue of affordability is the level of premium that will need to be charged. If this turns out to be very high, then the burden on workers would be intolerably high in low-income countries where wages are not much above subsistence levels. Similarly, the burden on enterprises and the market distortions arising from the introduction of the scheme would also be too high. In practice, however, all the evidence points to the fact that the required contribution rate is very low, ranging from 1 to 4 per cent of payroll. This emerges from the data presented in table 4.1 on the features of the unemployment insurance system in the thirteen developing countries that have such schemes. It is interesting to note that six of these countries have schemes that are entirely self-financing.

The question now arises as to whether there are any reasons to believe that the affordability problem is likely to be greater for the South-East and East Asian countries than for the countries shown in table 4.1. The answer is a clear no. Per capita incomes in the Asian countries are as high, if not higher, than in those countries with unemployment insurance (see table 4.2). Wages are also significantly higher than subsistence levels, so the modest payroll tax required can be borne without hardship. A key determinant of the required level of contributions is the ratio of claimants to contributors. A good proxy of this is average unemployment rate over the past five or ten years. Here, too, the South-East and East Asian countries are relatively well-placed. Their pre-crisis unemployment rates, as has already been noted, were extremely low and there is every reason to believe that the high current levels of unemployment will fall towards these trend levels once economic recovery is in full swing.

A recent feasibility study carried out by the ILO for Thailand,[21] provides detailed confirmation for supposing that the required contribution rate will be very modest. As shown in table 4.3, the required contribution rate for a scheme that pays benefits for six months at a level equal to 50 per cent of previous earnings would be 2.5 per cent of payroll in the first year of operation, but would fall steadily thereafter to 0.6 per cent by the seventh year. It should be noted that this rate allows for the accumulation of a reserve equivalent to one year's expenditure on benefits. The ILO

Table 4.1. Features of unemployment insurance in low- and middle-income countries

Country	First and current law	Coverage	Contributions Insured: % earnings	Employers: % payrolls	State	Minimum contribution	Reference earnings	Replacement ratio (%)	Length of benefits	Depending on:	Waiting period
Algeria	1994	Non-agriculture employees	1.5	2.5	None	3 years with 6 months prior to unemployment	Average monthly earnings	50 + 1/2 Min. wage	6-36 months	Contributions	None
Argentina	1967,91	Employed persons	1	1.5	None	1 year	Highest wage in the last 6 months	60	12-36 months	Contributions	None
Barbados	1982	Employees aged 16-64	1.5	1.5	None	1 year + 20 weeks prior to unemployment	Average weekly earnings	60	26 weeks		3 days
Brazil	1965,90	Employed persons	0	0	Whole cost	36 months in the last 4 years	Average earnings in the last 3 months	50	4 months		60 days
Chile	1937,81	Employed persons	0	0	Whole cost	52 weeks in the last 2 years	None	Fixed monthly sum	360 days		None
China	1986,93	Employees in state-run enterprises	0	0.6-1	Subsidies	1 year	Public assistance benefit	150-120	12-24 months	Contributions	None

Country	Year	Coverage			Government	Qualifying conditions	Benefit base	Rate	Duration	Variation factors	Waiting period
Ecuador	1951,88	Employed persons	2	1	None	24 months	Earnings and length of last employment	Lump sum	Indefinite		60 days
Egypt	1959,75	Private sector non-agriculture employees	0	2	Any deficit	6 months, with 3 of them consecutive	Last monthly wage	60	16-28 weeks	Contributions	7 days
Iran	1987,90	Salaried employees	0	3	Any deficit	6 consecutive months	Average earnings	80-55	6-50 months	Contributions and family status	None
South Africa	1937,96	Employees earning US$16,870 a year or less	1	1	None	13 weeks in the last year	Weekly earnings	45	26 weeks		7 days
Tunisia	1982	Non-agriculture salaried employees	0	0	Whole cost	12 quarters	Minimum wage	100	3 months		None
Uruguay	1944,81	Employees in industry and commerce	15-16[1]	12.5-15[1]	Not specified	6 months in the last year	Average earnings	60-50	n.a		None
Venezuela	1989	Employed persons	0.7	1.5	None	52 weeks in the last 2 years	Average weekly salary	60	13-26 weeks	Special circumstances	1 month

n.a. = not available.

[1] Overall contributions for social security.

Source: Social Security Administration (USA): *Social security programmes throughout the world*, 1997.

study also addressed the question of administrative feasibility, and found that the main requirement of such a scheme would be an increase in the staffing level of the employment service from its current 1,000 staff to 4,700. This would enable it to extend its geographical coverage and to take on new functions, the most demanding of which would be the prevention of fraudulent claims. This level of increase in staff is affordable and this additional cost has in fact been included in the calculation of the required rate of contribution shown in table 4.3. These figures for Thailand are in line with the actual contribution rates in the Republic of

Table 4.2. Economic indicators for low- and middle-income countries[1] operating an unemployment insurance programme for selected Asian countries (1995)

Country	GNP per capita (US$)	Non-agriculture GDP per employee (US$)	Social security expenditure (% of GDP)
Algeria	1 600		
Argentina	8 030	25 448	4.31
Barbados	6 560	14 551	5.23
Brazil	3 640	9 798	
Chile	4 160		22.67
China	620	1 844	2.55
Ecuador	1 390	5 279	2.08
Egypt	790	4 043	
Iran	2 200 [2]		0.94
South Africa	3 160		
Tunisia	1 820	4 249	5.68
Uruguay	5 170	14 163	
Venezuela	3 020	9 775	
Indonesia	980	3 164	0.06
Korea	9 700	15 429	2.18
Malaysia	3 890	10 777	0.15
Philippines	1 050	2 802	3.01
Thailand	2 740	5 962	0.12

[1] Low- and middle-income countries are defined as those whose GNP per capita is below US$10,000.   [2] 1992.

Sources: World Bank: *World Development Indicators*, 1997; ILO: *Yearbook of Labour Statistics*, 1997; ILO: *Cost of Social Security, Fifteenth International Inquiry*, 1997.

Korea since the introduction of its unemployment insurance scheme in 1995, where the contribution rate is 0.6 per cent of payroll, shared equally by employers and workers.[22]

Estimates have also been made of what the required contribution rate would have been in the Republic of Korea, Thailand and Indonesia had these countries introduced unemployment insurance in 1991, that is, six years before the onset of the crisis. These are shown in table 4.4. The main assumptions underlying these calculations are that the coverage of the scheme would be the same as for social security and would provide 12 months of benefit at a replacement rate of 50 per cent of previous earnings. All the most recently available data on actual flows into unemployment have been used for calculations, supplemented by projections of the impact of the crisis on unemployment. It is important to note that in this way the cost calculations have taken into account the effects of the sharp rise in benefit payments that would have been necessary as a consequence of the crisis-induced rise in unemployment. The striking result of these calculations is that an average required contribution rate of between 0.3 to 0.4 per cent of payroll from 1991 to 2000 would have been sufficient to provide all insured job losers over this period, including during the current crisis, with 12 months of benefits. This would have made a significant contribution to cushioning the harsh impact of the crisis on modern-sector workers.

Table 4.3. Thailand: Required contribution rate for an unemployment insurance scheme (% of payroll)

Year	Required rate (%)[1]
2001	2.5
2002	1.6
2003	1.3
2004	1.1
2005	0.8
2006	0.6
2007	0.6

[1] Rate required to maintain a contingency reserve of one annual expenditure.

Source: ILO: *Assessment of the feasibility*, op. cit.

Table 4.4. Thailand, Indonesia and the Republic of Korea:
Estimates of required annual contribution rate to finance
unemployment insurance 1991-2000 (% of payroll)

	1991-2000 (%)
Thailand	0.31
Indonesia	0.44
Republic of Korea	0.25

Contribution rates have been calculated using the following assumptions:

(1) In each year, the number of job losers has been calculated as the difference between the net inflow into unemployment minus the number of first-time job seekers.

(2) The net inflow into unemployment is defined as the annual variation in unemployment.

(3) The number of first-time job seekers has been estimated by multiplying the annual variation in the labour force by the unemployment rate in the same year (i.e. by the probability of a first-time job seeker remaining unemployed).

(4) Regarding the duration of unemployment, we have assumed that all job losers in 1997 were laid off in the second half of the year (i.e. when the crisis began to hit) and in that each subsequent year entry into unemployment occurred at a constant monthly rate.

(5) In Indonesia and Thailand – where unemployment benefits were not available at the onset of the crisis – we have assumed that the coverage of an unemployment insurance scheme would have been similar to existing social security programmes (sickness and invalidity benefits, health services, etc.). Therefore, the percentage of job losers entitled to benefits was assumed to equal the percentage of workers paying contributions to the SSO funds.

In the case of the Republic of Korea, the figures on the number of unemployed covered by the current unemployment scheme have been drawn from the 1998 Ministry of Labour's Report.

(6) For each year, the average level of monthly benefits has been assumed to equal 50% of average monthly wage.

(7) Contribution rates have been calculated under the assumption of a duration equal to one year.

Economic effects

A basic point to be made at the outset is that at the very modest levels of required contributions described above, the effects of unemployment insurance on labour costs and hence on the demand for labour would be negligible. Similarly, the level of benefits and their proposed duration are also modest. Thus, even if we concede the theoretical argument that there is a negative impact of payroll taxes and unemployment benefits on the level of employment, the empirical significance of this in the cases at hand is moot. More generally, the empirical evidence for the industrialized countries in support of the hypothesis that unemployment benefits have a negative impact on employment is not particularly compelling. Where a negative impact has been found, the magnitude involved is very small. On average these estimates imply that a 10 per cent increase in the replacement rate of unemployment benefit would be associated with an increase of only 1.5 weeks in the duration of unemployment.[23] Moreover, it should be noted that these results are for unemployment benefit systems that are significantly more generous than the scheme proposed here.

Indeed, many of the alleged negative effects of unemployment benefits do not apply to this type of scheme. Negative effects are strongest for a system based on the unconditional payment of a standard flat rate of benefits for the entire period of unemployment.[24]

The insurance system being proposed here differs radically in that it attaches a set of conditions to reduce the potential negative effects on unemployment. First, workers who quit their jobs voluntarily or who are dismissed for misconduct are not eligible for unemployment benefits. This eliminates problems arising from the fact that unemployment benefits would raise the incentives to quit or shirk and hence raise wage rates. Second, eligibility is tied to a period of previous contribution, thus avoiding the problem that unemployment benefits would raise the reservation wage of those who have not previously worked. Third, the limited duration of benefits reduces the negative impact that unemployment benefits may have on the willingness to seek work. This is reinforced by the condition that eligibility to benefits is linked to past contributions to the scheme: the only way workers nearing the end of their period of entitlement can requalify for future benefits is to return to work. Fourth, the moral hazard of a greater propensity to avoid work owing to the availability of benefits is greatly reduced by the requirement that benefit recipients must be actively engaged in job search and do not refuse suitable job offers.

Finally, it can be shown that an unemployment insurance scheme with limited benefits does not impose forced saving on workers and does not lead workers to demand a compensating wage premium.[25] As a result, neither the equilibrium wage rate nor the unemployment rate is affected by the introduction of unemployment insurance.

Another argument that has been advanced is that mandatory contributions to an unemployment insurance fund would lower the rate of private saving by reducing business profits and the margin for saving out of wages. This would thus reduce the rate of investment and hence growth. However, the empirical effect is in fact quite small. A cross-country regression run on sixty-five countries with the relevant data for 1995 showed that an increase of one percentage point in the ratio of social security taxes to GDP will cause a reduction of half a percentage point in the propensity to save.[26] Although not negligible, this is hardly a serious obstacle to the introduction of unemployment insurance for countries such as Thailand, Indonesia, the Republic of Korea, Malaysia, Singapore and Hong Kong, China, where gross domestic savings have been more than 30 per cent of GDP for a sustained period. They can thus easily absorb the very slight decline in savings that the introduction of mandatory contributions for unemployment insurance would provoke. Moreover, recalling that our earlier estimates of the required contribution rate showed this to be well below 1 per cent of GDP, the negative impact on growth resulting from the introduction of unemployment insurance will also be slight.

The claim has also been made that the administrative capacity to run an unemployment insurance scheme does not exist in developing countries. While this may be true for the least developed countries of the world, this is certainly not so for countries such as Thailand, Malaysia and Indonesia, where tertiary education has expanded rapidly and a large pool of skilled labour already exists. As was shown in the ILO feasibility study for Thailand,[27] the required expansion of administrative capacity to run an unemployment insurance scheme is relatively modest. The recent experience of the transition economies in the setting up of unemployment schemes further supports this: countries such as Hungary, Poland and the Czech Republic achieved a satisfactory level of operation of their unemployment insurance system within two years of their creation in 1990-91.[28]

Another long-standing objection is that the presence of a large proportion of informal employment precludes the introduction of unemployment insurance in developing countries. One reason given is that this makes universal coverage difficult to administer; the other is that the introduction of unemployment insurance in dualistic labour markets would harm economic development. The first objection does not apply to the type of scheme proposed here, which initially involves only wage employees in the modern sector. The rationale for this is set out at the beginning of this section. As to the second objection, a major counter-argument is that economic development is mainly driven by growth of income in the modern sector. By making modern-sector jobs more attractive, unemployment insurance will promote greater competition for such jobs and induce a more efficient allocation of labour and faster growth of the modern sector. This is not an insignificant consideration in such countries as Malaysia, Thailand and Singapore, where severe labour shortages were experienced in the immediate pre-crisis period. Concern that this emphasis on modern-sector growth would increase inequality between the modern and informal sectors is also misplaced. The pre-crisis performance of these economies has shown that such a modern-sector-led growth strategy has resulted in a rapid shrinking of the informal sector and a consequent reduction in poverty and decline in income inequality.

A final objection is that introducing unemployment insurance in the midst of a crisis would not be feasible. While it is true that initial costs of the scheme would be abnormally high, the experience of other countries in dealing with this problem is instructive. The solution has been to adopt a two-stage strategy.[29] The first stage involves running a deficit that future contributions during the recovery will absorb. The deficit could be kept low if initial benefits are confined to a minimal flat-rate payment applicable to all claimants. When economic conditions improve, the system can shift to the next stage where the level of benefits could progressively be raised and become more closely linked to past earnings and contributions. At the end of this transitional phase (i.e. when the initial deficit has been eliminated), the system could shift to normal insurance-based operations.

Social safety net

Although the introduction of unemployment insurance would be an important breakthrough it will not, of course, meet the needs of new entrants to the labour market and informal sector workers who lose their jobs. This is why it is important to take parallel action to develop a full-fledged social safety net. The ultimate objective should be to develop a means-tested social assistance that provides minimum income support. An interim measure would be to put in place a system of guaranteed employment in public projects for a subsistence wage. As discussed in Chapter 3, this would be a self-targeting measure since only those in dire need would seek such jobs. A critical requirement is to develop the capacity to rapidly scale-up such schemes to meet the vast increase in the demand for such assistance during periods of economic crisis.

4.5 CONCLUDING REMARKS

The sudden unravelling of the South-East and East Asian economic miracle has caused widespread misery and has imperilled social and political stability in the region. Millions who laboured to forge the miracle have become innocent and bewildered victims of the unfolding economic collapse. A human disaster of this scale is shocking to behold.

Repairing the economic damage requires action on many fronts, ranging from reforms to the international financial system to deep structural changes within the crisis-affected countries. Success on this front will rekindle economic growth, the ultimate basis for salving current social wounds and restoring social progress. But it would be foolhardy to ignore the lessons for social policy that have been so painfully driven home by the crisis. A fundamental rethinking on the social dimension of economic development is as important as the purely economic and financial issues that currently occupy centre stage.

This chapter, and indeed most of the book, has been an attempt to provoke and contribute to that rethinking. A new and better social contract is both desirable and feasible, even on narrow economic grounds. The moral case is no less powerful.

Notes and references

[1] ILO Freedom of Association and Protection of the Right to Organise Convention, 1948 (No. 87). See also Lee, 1998.

[2] Leary, 1996, p. 22.

[3] Sen, 1996, p. 154.

[4] ibid.

[5] See Lee, 1997.

[6] Sen, 1997, pp. 14-15.

[7] Li Xiaorong, 1998.

[8] ibid.

[9] Sen, op. cit., p. 15.

[10] ibid., p. 17.

[11] See Stephen Nickell: "Unemployment and labour market rigidities: Europe versus North America", in *Journal of Economic Perspectives*, Vol. 4, No. 3, Summer 1997, pp. 55-74. Robert M. Solow: *What is labour market flexibility? What is it good for?* (Royal Academy, London, 1997, Keynes Lecture). Alan B. Krueger and Jörn-Steffen Pischke: *Observations and conjecture on the US employment miracle*, NBER Working Paper No. 6146, August 1997.

[12] Mill, 1869.

[13] ibid.

[14] Sen, op. cit.

[15] Stiglitz, 1998f.

[16] Layard and Nickell, 1986, pp. S121-169.

[17] Stiglitz, 1985, pp. 595-618; Shapiro and Stiglitz, 1985, pp. 1215-1217.

[18] Hamermesh, 1992.

[19] Akerlof, 1970, pp. 488-500.

[20] Rothschild and Stiglitz, 1976, pp. 630-649.

[21] ILO, 1998b.

[22] ILO, 1998a, p. 41.

[23] See Moffit, 1985; Meyer, 1990, pp. 757-782.

[24] Atkinson and Micklewright, 1991, pp. 1679-1727.

[25] Spiezia, 1998.

[26] The estimated equation was:

Save = $-39.41 + 7.0* \ln y - .50 *Soc$ $F = 12.2$ $R^2 = .28$
  (−3.31) (4.93)   (−1.87)   T statistics in parenthesis

Where Save = ratio of domestic savings to GDP; ln y = log of per capita GDP; and Soc = ratio of social security taxes to GDP.

[27] ILO, 1998b.

[28] Boeri, 1997.

[29] Barr, 1994.

BIBLIOGRAPHY

Akerlof, G. 1970. "The market for 'lemons': Qualitative uncertainty and the market mechanism", in *Quarterly Journal of Economics*, Vol. LXXXIV, No. 3, August.

Alba, P.; Bhattacharya, A.; Claessens, S.; Ghosh, S.; Hernandez, L. 1998. *Volatility and contagion in a financially-integrated world: Lessons from East Asia's recent experience*, World Bank and Central Bank of Chile, paper presented at the PAFTAD 24 Conference on Asia Pacific Financial Liberalization and Reform, 20-22 May (Chiangmai, Thailand).

Asian Development Bank, Country Data, available on Website: http://internotes.asiandevbank.org/notes/edr0004p/Excel.htm.

Atkinson, A.B.; Micklewright, J. 1991. "Unemployment compensation and labor market transitions. A critical review", in *Journal of Economic Literature*, Vol. 29, No. 4, December, pp. 1679-1727.

Barr, N. 1994. "Income transfers: Social insurance", in Barr (ed): *Labour market and social policy in Central and Eastern Europe: The transition and beyond* (New York and Oxford, Oxford University Press).

Bello, W. 1998. *The end of the Asian miracle*, on Website: http://www.stern.nyu.edu/~nroubini/asia/miracle.pd. Retrieved in March 1998.

Bhagwati, J. 1998. "The capital myth: The difference between trade in widgets and dollars", in *Foreign Affairs*, May-June.

Boeri, T. 1997. "Labour market reforms in transition economies" in *Oxford Review of Economic Policy*, Vol. 13, No. 2, Summer.

Calvo, G.A.; Mendoza, E.G. 1998. *Rational herd behaviour and the globalization of securities markets*, on Website: http://www.econ.duke.edu/Papers/Abstracts97/abstract.97.26.html. Retrieved on 15 September 1998.

—; Leiderman, L.; Reinhart, C.M. 1996. "Inflows of capital to developing countries in the 1990s", in *Journal of Economic Perspectives*, Vol. 10, No. 2, Spring.

Camdessus, M. 1998a. *The IMF and its programs in Asia*, New York, 6 February. On Website: http://www.imf.org/external/np/speeches/1998/020698.htm. Retrieved on 9 February 1998.

—. 1998b. *Reflections on the crisis in Asia*, Caracas, Venezuela, 7 February. On Website: http://www.imf.org/external/np/speeches/1998/020798.htm. Retrieved on 18 February 1998.

Chang, H-J. 1998. "Korea: The misunderstood crisis", in *World Development*, Vol. 26, No. 8, August.

—; Park, H-J.; Yoo, C.G. 1998. "Interpreting the Korean crisis: Financial liberalisation, industrial policy and corporate governance", in *Cambridge Journal of Economics*, Vol. 22, No. 6, November.

Condon, T. 1998a. *South Korea: The terms of trade shock warrants monetary easing*, Morgan Stanley, in *Global Economic Forum*, on Website: http://www.ms.com/gef/. Retrieved in March 1998.

—. 1998b. "Malaysia: Capital controls", Morgan Stanley, in *Global Economic Forum*, on Website: http://www.ms.com/gef. Retrieved in September 1998.

Corbett, J.; Vines, D. 1998. *The Asian crisis: Competing explanations*, Center for Economic Policy Analysis (CEPA), CEPA Working Paper Series III, Working Paper No. 7, July, New York. On Website: http://www.newschool.edu/cepa/papers/archive/cepa0307.pdf. Retrieved on 16 September 1998.

Corsetti, G.; Pesenti, P.; Roubini, N. 1998. *Paper tigers? A preliminary assessment of the Asian crisis*, paper prepared for the NBER/Bank of Portugal International Seminar on Macroeconomics (ISOM), 14-15 June (Lisbon). On Website: http://www.stern.nyu.edu/~nroubini/asia/tiger04.pd. Retrieved on 16 September 1998.

Demirgüç-Kunt, A.; Detragiache E. 1998. *Financial liberalization and financial fragility*, International Monetary Fund, Working Paper No. 83, June. On Website: http://www.imf.org/external/pubs/ft/wp/wp9883.pdf. Retrieved on 16 September 1998.

Dooley, M.P. 1998. "The Tobin tax: Good theory, weak evidence, questionable policy", in M. ul Haq, I. Kaul and I. Grunberg (eds.): *The Tobin tax* (New York and Oxford, Oxford University Press).

Dornbusch, R. 1998a. *After Asia: New directions for the international financial system*, MIT, July, on Website: http://www.mit.edu/~rudi/papers.html. Retrieved on 16 September 1998.

—. 1998b. *Asian crisis themes*, MIT, February, on Website: http://www.mit.edu/~rudi/papers.html. Retrieved on 16 September 1998.

Esquivel, G.; Larraín, F.B. 1998. *Explaining currency crises*, paper presented at a Kennedy School of Government seminar, June (Harvard, Massachusetts).

Feldstein, M. 1998. "Refocusing the IMF: Overdoing it in East Asia", in *Foreign Affairs*, March-April.

Ferguson, R.W. 1998. *The Asian crisis. Lessons to be learned and relearned*, paper presented before America's Community Bankers, Washington, DC, 4 March. On Website: http://www.bog.frb.fed.us/boarddocs/speeches/. Retrieved on 5 March 1998.

Fischer, S. 1998a. *The Asian crisis: A view from the IMF*, 22 January. On Website: http://www.imf.org/external/np/speeches/1998/012298.htm. Retrieved on 23 January 1998.

—. 1998b. *The IMF and the Asian crisis*, Los Angeles, 20 March. On Website: http://www.imf.org/external/np/speeches/1998/032098.htm. Retrieved on 22 March 1998.

George, E.A.J. 1998. "Mr. George discusses the problems in Asia and considers the risks they pose to the global economy", in *Bank for International Settlements Review*, (5/1998). On Website: http://www.bis.org/review/index.htm. Retrieved on 5 February 1998.

Greenspan, A. 1998a. *Testimony of Chairman Alan Greenspan before the Committee on Banking and Financial Services, US House of Representatives, 30 January 1998*, on Website: http://www.bog.frb.fed.us/boarddocs/testimony/19980130.htm. Retrieved on 4 February 1998.

—. 1998b. *Remarks by Chairman Alan Greenspan before the Annual Convention of the Independent Bankers Association of America, Honolulu, Hawaii, 3 March 1998*, on Website: http://www.bog.frb.fed.us/boarddocs/speeches/. Retrieved on 5 March 1998.

Grenville, S. 1997. "Asia and the financial sector", in *Bank of Australia Bulletin*. On Website: http://www.rba.gov.au/bulletin/bu_dec97/bu_sp_dg_0412.pdf. Retrieved in December 1997.

—. 1998a. "Mr. Grenville discusses exchange rates and crises against the background of the financial turmoil in Asia", in *Bank for International Settlements Review* (13/1998) On Website: http://www.bis.org/review/index.htm. Retrieved on 27 February 1998.

—. 1998b. *The Asian economic crisis*, paper presented at a talk to Australian Business Economists and the Economic Society of Australia, Sydney, 12 March. On Website: http://www.rba.gov.au/speech/sp_dg_1203.html. Retrieved on 12 March 1998.

Hamermesh, D.S. 1992. "Unemployment insurance for developing countries", in *Policy Research Working Papers: Education and employment 897*, World Bank, Population and Human Resources Department.

ILO (International Labour Office). 1997a. *Yearbook of Labour Statistics* (Geneva).

—. 1997b. *World Labour Report 1997-98* (Geneva).

—. 1998a. *The social impact of the Asian financial crisis*, April (Bangkok).

—. 1998b. *Assessment of the feasibility of introducing an unemployment insurance scheme in Thailand* (Geneva), July, mimeo.

ILO/UNDP. 1998. *Employment challenges of the Indonesian economic crisis*, June (Jakarta).

IMF (International Monetary Fund). 1998. *World economic outlook*, October (Washington, DC).

Kapur, A. 1998. "Resolving Asia's crisis: The IMF way and the right way", UBS Global Research, in *Asian Equities Weekly*, 15-21 January.

Krugman, P. 1998a. *What happened to Asia?* On Website: http://web.mit.edu/krugman/www/. Retrieved on 12 January 1998.

—. 1998b. *Currency crises*. On Website: http://web.mit.edu/krugman/www/. Retrieved on 12 January 1998.

—. 1998c. *Asia: What went wrong*. On Website: http://web.mit.edu/krugman/www/. Retrieved on 19 February 1998.

—. 1998d. *Fire-sale FDI*. On Website: http://web.mit.edu/krugman/www/. Retrieved on 19 February 1998.

—. 1998e. *Will Asia bounce back?*. On Website: http://web.mit.edu/krugman/www/. Retrieved on 24 March 1998.

—. 1998f. "Saving Asia: It's time to get radical", in *Fortune Investor*, September, on Website: http://www.pathfinder.com/fortune/investor/1998/980907/sol.html. Retrieved on 16 September 1998.

Layard, R.; Nickell, S. 1986. "Unemployment in Britain", *Economica*, Vol. 53, Supplement.

Leary, V.A. 1996. "The paradox of workers' rights as human rights", in Lance A. Compa and Stephen F. Diamond: *Human rights, labour rights, and international trade* (Philadelphia, University of Pennsylvania Press).

Lee, E. 1997. "Globalization and labour standards: A review of issues", in *International Labour Review*, Vol. 136, No. 2.

—. 1998. "Trade union rights: An economic perspective", in *International Labour Review*, Vol. 137, No. 3.

Li Xiaorong. 1998. *A question of priorities: Human rights, development, and Asian values* (Institute for Philosophy and Public Policy, 1998).

Litan, R.E. 1998. "A three-step remedy for Asia's financial flu", in *Brookings Policy Brief Series*, No. 30. On Website: http://www.brook.edu/es/policy/policy.htm. Retrieved on 19 February 1998.

Macfarlane, I.J. 1997. "The changing nature of economic crises", in *Reserve Bank of Australia Bulletin*. On Website: http://www.rba.gov.au/bulletin/bu_dec97/bu_sp_gov_0412.pdf. Retrieved in December 1997.

McKinnon, R.I. 1998a. *The IMF, the East Asian currency crisis, and the world dollar standard*, paper prepared for the American Economic Association 1998 Annual Meetings, 3-5 January (Chicago, Illinois).

—. 1998b. *Exchange rate coordination for surmounting the East Asian currency crisis*, keynote speech presented at the 6th Convention of the East Asian Economic Association, 4-5 September (Kitakyushu, Japan).

Meyer, B.D. 1990. "Unemployment insurance and unemployment spells" in *Econometrica*, Vol. 58, No. 4.

Mill, J.S. 1869. "Thornton on labour and its claims: Part II", in *Fortnightly Review*, June.

Moffit, R. 1985. "Unemployment insurance and the distribution of unemployment spells", in *Journal of Econometrics*, Vol. 28, No. 1.

Montes, M. F. 1998. *The currency crisis in Southeast Asia* (Singapore, Institute of Southeast Asian Studies).

Obstfeld, M. 1998. *The global capital market: Benefactor or menace?*, National Bureau of Economic Research, NBER Working Paper No. 6559, May, on Website: http://www.nber.org/papers/w6559. Retrieved on 16 September 1998.

Park, Y.C.; Song, C-Y. 1998. *The East Asian financial crisis: A year later*, paper presented to East Asian Workshop at the Institute of Development Studies at the University of Sussex, 13 July.

Polanyi, K. 1957. *The great transformation* (Boston, Beacon Press).

Rodrik, D. 1998. *Who needs capital-account convertibility?*, Harvard University, February, paper written as contribution to a symposium edited by Peter Kenen (to be published as part of a "Princeton Essay in International Finance"). On Website: http://www.nber.org/~drodrik/essay.PDF. Retrieved on 16 September 1998.

Rothschild, M.; Stiglitz, J. 1976. "Equilibrium in competitive insurance markets: An essay on the economics of imperfect information", in *Quarterly Journal of Economics*, Vol. XC, No. 4, November.

Sachs, J. 1997. "The wrong medicine for Asia", in *The New York Times*, 3 November.

—. 1998. "To stop the money panic", in *Asia Week Online*, 13 February. On Website: http://www.pathfinder.com/asiaweek/. Retrieved on 23 February 1998.

—. Radlet, S. 1998. *The onset of the East Asian financial crisis*, First draft, 10 February. On Website:
http://www.hiid.harvard.edu/pub/other/eaonset.pdf. Retrieved on February 1998.

Sen, A. 1996. "Legal rights and moral rights: Old questions and new problems", in *Ration Juris*, Vol. 9, No. 2, June.

—. 1997. *Development thinking at the beginning of the 21st century* (London School of Economics, STICERD Development Economics Research Programme, Working Paper No. 2, March).

Shapiro, C.; Stiglitz, J.E. 1984. "Unemployment equilibrium as a worker discipline device", in *American Economic Review*, Vol. 74, No. 3, June.

Singapore Government. 1998. *1998 Budget Statement*, 31 March.

Social Security Administration (SA). 1997. *Social security programmes throughout the world*, Research Report No. 65, SSA publication No. 13-11805, August (Washington, DC).

Spiezia, V. 1998. "The effect of unemployment insurance on employment and wage" (ILO, Cross-Departmental Analyses and Reports Team, mimeo).

Stiglitz, J.E. 1985. "Equilibrium wage distributions", in *Economic Journal*, Vol. 95, No. 379, September.

—. 1997. "How to fix the Asian economies", in *New York Times*, 31 October.

—. 1998a. "More instruments and broader goals: Moving towards the post-Washington consensus", 1998 WIDER Annual Lecture (Helsinki, Finland), 7 January.

—. 1998b. "Bad private-sector decisions", in *Wall Street Journal*, 4 February.

—. 1998c. *The role of international financial institutions in the current global economy*, Address to the Council of Foreign Relations, 27 February (Chicago). On Website: http://www.worldbank.org/html/extdr/extme/jssp022798.htm. Retrieved on 10 March 1998.

—. 1998d. *Knowledge for development: Economic science, economic policy and economic advice*, address to the World Bank's 10th Annual Bank Conference on Development Economics (ABCDE), Washington, DC, on Website: http://www.worldbank.org/html/extdr/extme/js-abcde98/js_abcde98.htm. Retrieved on 16 September 1998.

—. 1998e. *The East Asian crisis and its implications for India*, Commemorative Lecture for the Golden Jubilee Year Celebration of the Industrial Finance Corporation of India, New Delhi, 19 May. On Website: http://www.worldbank.org/html/extdr/extme/js-051998/default.htm. Retrieved on 16 September 1998.

—. 1998f. *Distribution, efficiency and voices: Designing the second generation of reforms* (World Bank, July, mimeo, Washington DC). On Website http://www.worldbank.org/html/extdr/extme/jssp071498.htm.

Summers, L.H. 1998. *Deputy Secretary Summers remarks before the International Monetary Fund, 9 March 1998*. On Website: http://www.treas.gov/press/releases/pr2286.htm. Retrieved on 22 March 1998.

Taylor, L. 1998. *Lax public sector, destabilizing private sector: Origins of capital market crises*, Center for Economic Policy Analysis (CEPA), CEPA Working Paper Series III, Working Paper No. 6, July (New York). On Website: http://www.newschool.edu/cepa/papers/archive/cepa0306.pdf. Retrieved on 16 September 1998.

Wade, R. 1998a. *The Asian debt-and-development crisis of 1997-?: Causes and consequences*, on Website: http://tap.epn.org/sage/asia698.html. Retrieved on 16 September 1998.

—. 1998b. *From miracle to meltdown: Vulnerabilities, moral hazard, or panic and debt deflation in the Asian crisis?*, on Website: http://tap.epn.org/sage/asiac3a.html. Retrieved on 16 September 1998.

Warburg Dillon Read. 1998. *Asian Adviser*, 7 September.

—. 1998. *Asian Adviser Daily*, 17 September.

Wolf, M. 1998. "Caging the bankers", in *The Financial Times*, 20 January 1998.

—; Veneroso, F. 1998. "The Asian crisis: The high debt model vs. the Wall Street-Treasury-IMF Complex", in *New Left Review*, March-April 1998. On Website: http://tap.epn.org/sage/imf698.html. Retrieved on 16 September 1998.

World Bank. *World Development Indicators*, World Bank, Washington, DC.

Wyplosz, C. 1998. *Globalized financial markets and financial crises*, paper presented at the Conference on Coping with Financial Crises in Developing Countries: Regulatory and Supervisory Challenges in a New Era of Global Finance, Amsterdam, 16-17 March (Forum on Debt and Development). On Website: http://heiwww.unige.ch/~wyplosz/fondad.pdf. Retrieved on 16 September 1998.